Sins of the Fathers

I0099815

Fred Bailey

chipmunkapublishing
the mental health publisher

Published by
Chipmunkapublishing
PO Box 6872
Brentwood
Essex CM13 1ZT
United Kingdom

http://www.chipmunkapublishing.com

Edited by Aleks Lech

Chipmunkapublishing gratefully acknowledge the support of Arts Council England.

"As the twig is bent, so grows the tree" ...Alexander Pope

Fred Bailey

Author Biography

Fred Bailey was born in Hamilton, Southern Ontario in 1952. In that era, mental illness and emotional disorders were issues that were never openly discussed. A massive stigma was attached to a subject which was misunderstood even by the medical profession. Both parents were severely bi-polar; something he would not understand until near middle-age when he began to address the reckoning of his own health issues. Part of the therapy prescribed was to write about his feelings and memories, a process that eventually lead to a life as a writer. Bailey has now completed several literary works including two novels. He continues to write and supports his passion for writing and for sailing by working as a professional in various marine trades.

Preface

Sins of the Fathers

She is long gone now. We buried her on New Year's Eve, Almost seven years ago. There was fresh snow that morning in the Okanogan and the cemetery workers were leaving at noon. They had things to celebrate. The service was at eight A.M. and that gave some relatives an easy out; it was too early. I haven't heard from any of them since, nor they from me.

I began to write this book many years ago, just after my father had died. I travelled to the old hometown in Southern Ontario and put his affairs in order when the doctors called to say he was dying. I was the eldest son and it had been twenty-six years since I had last set foot there. That, in itself, says a lot. I did my duty, and also ripped open some long-festering wounds in the ordeal. After returning to my west coast home I waited several weeks until he finally died. A chapter in my life had closed and in catharsis I wrote furiously about a life spawned by two severely and similarly warped personalities.

It is, in fact, because of the immensely dysfunctional childhood I experienced that I began to write. It was prescribed as an excellent therapy and I have resolved a great many issues simply through the tangible recording, and then analysis, of so damned many painful recollections. I cannot explain what value there is to hold a printed page and say to oneself, 'Yes, that is so. That's the way I remember it happening. It was not my fault and yes, I have tried to rise to a higher self despite all of the negative programming.' Or: 'No! This is bullshit. I am merely inventing excuses for my frailty.'

Either way, all I know is that for me, it has often

worked. I recommend the process of objective, honest self-analysis. Write it down, and see if it sticks to the wall.

Something, however, held me back from writing freely, with frankness and without inhibition. It was my mother. For her entire life she had been a frustrating enigma to all who would try to love her. In her last years she was institutionalized and was finally forced, with the aid of some wonderful medications, to accept other people's affections, and on their terms. Finally my sister and I were able to love her without rejection. That my entire, life-long, fucked-up relationship with my mother ended so positively seems a miracle.

Cancer took her. She had spent most of her life in deliberate misery. She imposed on herself a life-long penance toward the day when she 'could be with Jesus, beyond this veil of tears.' However, when she realized that her toes were wet in the river she had so longed to cross, she began to fight to live. Finally, two years later, she lay back exhausted and apparently in peace. I can remember how her eyes became a clear aqua blue, and how she looked into mine of the same colour. She held my hand in both of hers and whispered, "Thank you." Those were the final words she spoke to either of her children. A week later, with my sister sitting by her bedside, mother died in her sleep. I remember her funeral and reading the eulogy I had written. I stood in front of the small group of mourners and realized that now I could rewrite the book. After seventeen years, my thoughts have fermented until this moment.

I dedicate this work to all of those who have endured similar and worse childhoods and live in shadow all of their days, too crushed to reach out for their true potential. Know that all things are possible for anyone if you dare to dream.

Introduction

A psychiatrist I once met joked about starting a support group for survivors of functional families. Her point was that it has become fashionable for many people to claim to have an abusive history and to come from a dysfunctional home. Most, however, have not actually been victimized, at least not as they think they have.

A new millennium is well under way. Western culture has never been so decadent. With that easy life comes ridiculously high personal expectations. If our fantasies are not met immediately, we are inclined to feel cheated and abused. Bombarded and seduced by the media, we are persuaded to believe that our lives should be just as perfect as those fabricated on the glossy page or the shining screen. Many in our culture demand pity because life is not fair and their concept of fairness is to have whatever one wants immediately.

Even so, the real world *is* full of real victims and real villains. That is the problem. Those genuinely abused are often brushed aside. Their plight is de-legitimized by the popular vogue to claim a history of deprivation or brutalization. Often, actual victims suffer on throughout their life, too diminished in spirit to demand recognition of the crushing childhood they have indeed endured. They will not, or cannot, find the help or solace that could make life a little more bearable. Often the basic test for the genuine victim of an abusive childhood is that they often blame themselves for their misery while the 'wannabe' blames everyone else.

Visit a third world country and meet the locals, not the ones working in the resorts and the glittering downtown shops, but those living in the backwaters, sometimes as close as a block from the main street. Despite severe deprivation, grave illnesses and desperate, apparently hopeless poverty, these people are usually able to look you clearly in the eye and offer a smile that comes from the bottom of their soul. Their lives are consumed with the basics of survival. God knows what sort of childhood they endured.

Most of our hectic agendas deal with everything *but* physical survival, which we arrogantly take for granted. When is the last time you worried about where you might find the next meal for yourself; or your children? The last time you were ill, or injured, did you wonder how you could possibly afford medical treatment, from any doctor? Were you annoyed that you couldn't see *your* family doctor, and as soon as you'd like? School? Housing? How little we know about basics! The difference between the third world perspective and ours are simply levels of expectation. Joy, or at least contentment, has little to do with a fiscal state.

There *are* things as certain as death and taxes. One is that life is not fair, whatever our perception of fairness may be. Another is that no one has a birthright to happiness. Few of us can actually verbalize our concept of happiness; the notions of it range between a simple ease of suffering to a state of supreme bliss. Probably the simplest definition is that it is the antithesis of unhappiness. For many living in our western culture, unhappiness is being at a material station beneath that of our expectations. That materialistic craving is often a substitute for self-love, personal fulfillment and all manner of phobias and guilt imposed on us by a consumer society gone mad. I have, therefore I am. Can we ever be happy? When is enough, enough? For many of us - never.

This raises a question about sanity. What does it mean to be sane? Dictionaries are vague and cautious with the definition. Does sanity mean conforming to the standards and accepting the values of the community we live in? In some societies, being a cannibal is accepted and even expected. In our culture that practice is regarded as an extreme example of madness. At least, that is, the *physical* consumption of one by another. What about moral, emotional and spiritual cannibalism? What if the culture we live in is indeed mad, and *not* conforming to its standards is sanity? Who decides? Who sets the standards? Who and what directs the status quo? To not conform does not necessarily mean that one is unbalanced. In fact, often the opposite may be true.

Perhaps a simple guideline to consider is if a person's values and endeavours have anything to do with immediate or long term survival and well being. Or, are they in fact harmful? In other words, if thinking people indulge in anything which will ultimately do themselves or others harm, is that insanity? If that is so, then God help us, we certainly live in a world filled with madness.

A rational baseline to determine if what we do makes sense and relates to any tangible value is a simple question. Does it have anything to do with someone to love, something to do or something to look forward to? There is really not anything else in our existence outside of those three things. All else is distraction. Most of us spend an enormous amount of our lives in desperate pursuit of distraction and take for granted these three components of human life.

We have become confused about our lives. (Who of us are not?) We are frustrated, often abusive and demanding, subjugating whomever it is easiest to overpower. Usually that person will be someone who wants only to love us and to be loved reciprocally. They are vulnerable, tolerant, dependent; they are the people who happen to be closest to us when we lash out in frustration. Those whom we need the most are the ones whom we abuse most vigorously. That is our nature. We assimilate the behaviour we learned by example while children, passing on the legacy of that dysfunction to the next generation who in turn pass it on yet again. That learned behaviour of abusiveness continues physically, emotionally and psychologically toward ourselves and the society that supposedly nurtures us.

Is behavioural and emotional dysfunction a product of nurture or of nature? Yes, to both. Each component of biological personality is impacted by learned behaviour and vice versa. Have you ever considered the habits and mannerisms of our parents and also of our children which irk us most? Aren't these the same personal traits which we possess and despise?

A good part of our collective panic and anger is due to the rate of change in our environment. We cannot assimilate the rapid evolution of our culture, the technical, the social, and the emotional. Life continues to move along at an ever-accelerating pace. We live with the pervasive pressure of a sense of uncertainty. Not so long ago parents raised their children in a world that had been essentially the same for their grandparents and, they expected, would probably be so for their great grandchildren. They held a tangible sense of where they were and who they were. How do we prepare our children now to live in a world that we cannot even imagine? Perhaps that is an explanation for our enduring need for medieval religions in a modern age. Be it a quest of the metaphysical, the environmental or the material, there is a need for a datum of permanence as we acknowledge our smallness within the cosmos.

We know, however, that at any point in history man has always abused and subjugated his fellow (often in the name of state and/or religion). Insecurity is not simply the effect of our modern frantic pace. One race or generation over another, one culture over another, one spouse over another, brothers, sisters, children, parents, kings and priests, we have always been bullies and are brutally selfish, both physically and psychologically. There are no easy answers as to why we are this way. We continue to live within the ruts of our selfish and destructive patterns of behaviour, even though we know, intellectually and spiritually, that we are destroying the only planet we can presently call our home.

"Sins of the Fathers" is not a supplication for pity of the protagonist. It is an account based on real events about a man who at middle age is still able to seek, and to sometimes find, glimmers of hope and humour. There are fragments of happy memory within the horror and shambles of a life that was inexorably shaped and permanently mutated by two severely dysfunctional personalities, his parents. The characters in this story are fictionalized, but the setting is real enough. Most of the events described *did* happen and are *still* happening somewhere. *'Fact is stranger than fiction'*. Sadly, as bizarre as some of the events in this story may be, there are many who suffer evil considerably deeper and darker. They endure unspeakable cruelties at this very moment, in your community, on your street, maybe even in your home.

This is an account as much about coping with an arduous childhood and its permanent effects, as it is an essay about a rapidly evolving society that moves from one era to another so quickly it is difficult for anyone to assimilate what is passing. We may well mourn the death of the extended family. In our culture people from previous generations are abandoned like dinosaurs. Their succeeding progeny alienate themselves, apparently caring little about ancestral wisdom and values.

One of the darker aspects of being abused, especially for a child, is the belief that no one else could possibly know what you endure. You truly believe that you have done something to deserve your lot in life. It is a sense of utter loneliness and worthlessness. You carry a load of guilt, suspicion and depression within yourself through your entire life. It is *not* merely an attitude. It is a tangible chemical-electrical fact of life as inexorable as the need to breath. Continually finding ways to punish yourself, you deny and defer happiness and any success that is available throughout your entire life. You plod eternally through an existence filled with regrets and misery, convinced that peace, happiness and love will never be yours. Sometimes, the story ends in suicide, either quick and dramatic, or drawn out through the misery of addiction and substance abuse. The pain that is unwittingly and selfishly transferred to others by survivors of abuse also has far reaching negative effects that will descend through successive generations.

How do we prevent the psychological battering of children? Where do we stop passing the buck? Is the parent abusive because he or she was abused? Whom do we charge with the original sin of the father? What about those who are aware of the abuse and choose to ignore it? Surely they too are responsible? Somewhere, sometime, someone will have to take personal responsibility.

Ultimately the only way of dealing with this sort of trauma is by acknowledging three things.
One: it did happen.
Two: it was not your fault.
Three: you have scars.
Accept them, learn to live with them, get on with your life. There is no point in blaming those whose weakness helped shape your own human frailty. They may well have suffered even more than you and in their way, as perverse as it may have been, they may well have done their best with what was available to them.

There is, however, a danger in moralizing. A person who truly suffers from clinical depression is often regarded as someone with inferior moral fibre. In fact, to endure a life that is saddled with this curse is possibly a strange way of *building* character. Perhaps that is why so many prominent personalities throughout history were people who suffered from permanent or recurring depression. We can explore libraries full of literature about depression, its causes and effects, but anaylsis is only beneficial if it leads to curative action.

You are who you are and, if you do not like that person, only you can make a change. You must first acknowledge the problem, then get the support you need. There are plenty of people in the business of providing help, but you must go to them. Acknowledging a problem is easily half of the solution. But nothing will happen until you do something!

Perhaps one can even find the courage to reach out and touch another person in similar circumstances. There is great healing in providing empathy and support from one's personal experience. Those who make the greatest contributions to society are people who have suffered most. That is why individuals and certain races are renowned for their musical heritage, their cultural, spiritual or financial leadership and their ability to continue to survive and thrive despite, or perhaps because of, unspeakable atrocities against them. The surest way to guarantee the continuance and rise of human spirit is to suppress it. The ability to endure pain is a sign of growth. Accept it. Know that only those who feel no pain are the dead.

Life is a fleeting thing. It is precious, fragile, and temporal. Just as we begin to grasp its greatness and an inkling of some of its meaning, we must acknowledge our frailty and insignificance, our mortality. We must embrace life because ultimately, all we have is *this* moment.

Chapter 1

Going Home

My name is Fred. I write with the sincere hope that perhaps someone can benefit from this work. My life would have been much easier if I had understood that I was not unique in my situation and impediments. Knowing that one thing would have meant so much. If only I can do that for another. How indelible are those memories of the dark eternities in my youth when all appeared to be a certainty of hopelessness and utter loneliness.

It was twenty-six years since I had last seen Oakville, my former home town on the shores of Lake Ontario, thirty years since I'd left my father's house. Now I was going back. My father was dying. As the eldest son, I was returning to put his affairs in order. I felt that I should; it was the tired cliché about the messy job that somebody has to do. I was not looking forward to the trip. The family was severely dysfunctional from my earliest memory and had exploded long ago. The fragments of that cataclysm had all blown west to British Columbia, as far away from dad as we could go without leaving the country. We had left him to his own devices and he had not improved with age.

Owing him nothing except a nagging urge for vindication, I realized that this would be my last opportunity to interact with him in any way. It was a final chance for interaction and absolution for us both. However things turned out, at least I would have made the effort. I would not go through the rest of my life with guilt about having done nothing when there was yet a possibility. My sister and my brother were not able, nor much interested, in becoming involved. He had hurt us all; deeply. I understand their reticence.

Sometimes years passed during which dad did not reciprocate any of our attempts to communicate. Then would come a sudden frenzied burst of letters and gifts. For example, passionate about steam trains, he did not understand that we were not and would shower us with gifts of calendars, books and recordings of railway sound effects. They would arrive without warning or any explanation, and his random benevolence, if not dealt with cautiously, would result in yet another fiasco.

Other times, letters would arrive claiming wild romantic exploits, sinister plots against him, chronic illness or disjointed, angry threats. Once he circulated letters among the family letter which were presented as being written by a second party and offering condolences for my father's suicide. The letters stated he had hung himself from the center-span of a local bridge. Amusingly, the handwriting was clearly that of my father. Later, he would deny any knowledge of the letters, claiming them to be proof of yet another anonymous scheme to discredit him. He often claimed an absolute memory loss in regard to each of his bizarre and ongoing heinous acts. Mother referred to them as his 'blackouts'.

Friends who knew bits of my past counselled me not to, 'waste time on the old bastard'. I could hear him repeatedly telling me as a youngster, 'You've made your bed, now bloody lie in it!' Although only one of many memories would be sufficient to justify leaving him alone, still my conscience badgered me. It was time to be the big brother, to assume my position as head of the family, to exploit the situation so that I could feel that I had done everything possible. After all, you usually only regret what you don't do and I have regrets enough already. Expecting an ordeal, my dread was nevertheless tinged with an eagerness to once again see the place of my youth. And so, early in May, a few days from my forty-fifth birthday I finally went home.

Sitting in the airport waiting to board my flight, I soon realized that it would be a long journey. I knew that the charter flight had been solidly booked. A private pilot, I hate to ride the airlines, especially when crammed into the narrow seat of an economy flight. As the waiting area filled with other passengers, seven Muslim men tended to their midday prayers. They took individual turns bowing and mumbling, for some reason each in a different direction, as their colleagues stood looking about stealthily and fiercely. Why did they appear so furtive and shifty? Why were they seven in number and were they really going to be on the same flight? Akmed and the Prayer-Boys: were they terrorists or just a band of surly-looking musicians who did not know where Mecca lay?

As it turned out there was no problem at all with the disoriented devout. I had been assigned a window seat on the flight and as luck would have it two other large men occupied the middle and aisle seats. I was trapped, knees around my ears, for the better part of four hours. At that time I worked on west coast tugboats and had just finished three long weeks at sea the day before this flight. I was setting out on a journey already exhausted, badly in need of a rest away from the confinement and regimentation of a small working vessel. The restriction of the economy-class seat was an agony.

Most of the way across the country, the air was clear and the earth raced past far beneath. I was dismayed at the brown monotony of the prairies and how every bit of them, to the horizon, seemed ploughed and organized into various square patterns of possession and exploitation. I already missed the wildness of the mountains and the ocean, only an hour behind me. Wherever I travel or stop for a while, my true home will always be the Canadian West Coast.

Soon the desolation of Northern Ontario slid beneath my window and once again I was over the country where I'd had many happy experiences as a young apprentice helicopter mechanic. Was that hopeful time of my life really a quarter-century in the past? The aircraft flew on into gathering gloom over some cloud cover and then under a great arching dome of blackness that was the visible edge of night. It was an eerie visual experience which left me feeling my smallness as I measured it against the universe around, above and beneath me. Even the huge Boeing in which I sat was just a faint whisper and a tiny flashing light passing slowly across the night sky, beneath countless galaxies of stars and the faint glimmer of undiscovered worlds. Did my life and that of my family mean anything?

We slipped beneath the cloud layer and the shining waters of Lake Superior appeared. I recognized the dark silhouette of Michipicoten Island. Soon after, the lights of Sault Saint Marie passed by, then Sudbury and in the distance North Bay lay beyond the outline of Lake Nipissing. The flight began descending over Lake Simcoe into an appalling solid blaze of light extending south to the shores of Lake Ontario. Suburbia and industry had consumed the entire country-side. Southern Ontario appeared to be one big city. The rural country and the farms of my childhood were gone forever.

My neck was cramped from peering out of the low window, it was a relief to finally go and stand in the line-up for the washroom. A young man urgently pushed ahead of me. He looked distressed. I did not make an issue of his rudeness. Ten minutes later, as the aircraft made its final approach to the Toronto airport, this same character was in the middle of a drug-overdose, almost flying himself around inside the aircraft. He held everyone's contempt. In fact, as the passengers sat trapped in their seats waiting in the parked aircraft for police and paramedics to pack the miscreant away, it was amazing to witness the gracious restraint of my fellow two hundred and twenty-seven tired, cramped, hot and impatient travellers. The hubbub and disorientation of the airport terminal was a relief after our claustrophobic wait. As usual, my bag was the last to appear on the luggage conveyor.

I expected to get lost driving from the airport to Oakville. It had, after all, been a quarter of a century. Warned about myriad changes and the confusing maze of freeways and interchanges, I was prepared to find myself well on the way toward Montreal before getting sorted out. Instead, the highways were remarkably well marked and I was driving into Oakville in only a few minutes. As a boy it had been nearly a half-day bicycle ride through many rural miles to the then named Malton Airport.

Incredibly, I still knew exactly where I was, everything falling into place as if all the years were no more than a day. I drove around town in the dark, along the same streets that I had wandered so long ago, alone and cold, peering into the warm light of other people's houses, wondering what having a normal life might be like. Thirty years later, I still wondered. It was amazing to be able to remember streets and the names of people who had lived, and perhaps still did, in homes that I recognized. It was startling to see how little had changed; the only thing that seemed radically different was that the scale of things and distances all seemed smaller. Sixteen Mile Creek that runs through Oakville had once seemed to me to a canyon-deep river. Now it was just a muddy stream in a shallow ditch. Living among mountains had changed my perceptions.

The two radio stations that I had listened to as a teenager were still playing the same music. CHUM 1050 in Toronto was now playing 'Golden Oldies', the very songs it had aired as the latest outrageous hits twenty-five years ago. The local radio station, CHWO '1250 on your dial - White Oak Radio', was yet airing the same schmaltzy champagne tunes. Lawrence Welk lived on in Oakville. I smiled to myself as a childhood memory came to mind. The radio station was then located on the upper floor of a small downtown brick building. My family had an old round-topped, wooden cabinet radio. I can still smell the hot dust on its tubes as they warmed up and began to glow. At that time I knew nothing of records and tapes. In childish innocence I listened to the radio intently between pieces of music, eternally disappointed that I never heard any sound as each new orchestra moved into that tiny building to play the next song. I actually believed that there was a constant stream of live musicians lugging their instruments in and out of radio stations all over the country.

My family listened daily to the 'CBC Six O'clock Evening News: As read by Walter Bowls' every suppertime. A solo jazz guitar was played as introduction to the newscast. Even to this day, I remember that tune each time I hear similar music. I used to marvel that some poor guy had to show up every night at the exact same time and play the same old tune. Just after lunch each day CBC aired a short children's program called 'Teddy Bear Picnic' and it was introduced with a tune of the same name. Today, whenever I hear it, there is a brief wave of drowsiness; a nap was on my childhood agenda after the program ended. The subliminal, insidious, indelible programming one receives as a child lasts a lifetime, whether administered deliberately or innocently, electronically or personally.

Now I was touring around my old hometown at midnight, tired, hungry, and with no place to go; something else that hadn't changed! It was amazing how little accommodation there was in the town and it was hard to find a room.

Morning broke clear and sparkling, cool and bright, a perfect spring day. A short stroll down the road from the motel brought me to a familiar address. I had once lived in this industrial building, sleeping on the floor of the lunchroom. During the daytime I served my apprenticeship as a helicopter mechanic. With a salary of forty-five dollars per week, I had very little money. Since I was soon being sent to a job-site somewhere in the great white Canadian North, there was no point in renting accommodation. So I bedded down in the hangar for a few weeks.

Outside, in this very spot was where I'd parked my first car. A 1958 Vauxhall Victor, or what was left of one. It was badly rusted, its floor long-gone and patched with bits of plywood. A worn engine belched blue, oily smoke. A weary suspension led the vehicle down the road like a crippled dog. The car's steering incessantly pulled to the left apparently in determination to end its pain in a head-on collision. Stopping the wreck required a furious pumping of the brake pedal each time. Fortunately there was not enough power left in its wheezing cylinders to attain any dangerous speeds. I had driven it for two years until it finally expired. I traded the wreck for two cases of beer.

Today this place was a semi-abandoned industrial storage site but in my memory I could yet smell aviation fuel, jet exhaust, parts-cleaning chemicals, and hear the exciting whine of a jet engine starting and the clatter of rotors. I began to remember faces and names of men with whom I had worked, and I wondered what had become of them. Once my father had learned that I worked here, he consistently plagued my employer with inquiries about where I was and what I was doing, all the while offering anecdotes from his imagination and warped memory about my childhood. He was the prime reason that I quit the job and moved as far away as I could. This day, it was time to move on again.

A while later I walked into the local hospital, soon finding myself standing beside my dying father's bed. At first I did not recognize him. He was asleep and I stood looking at him through a blur of tears. It had been twelve years since I last saw him, when he came to visit me in British Columbia. He had been active and healthy (albeit mad), and still had an enthusiasm for life in his peculiar way. Now he was a tired old relic, his hair turned snowy white, and with bushy whiskers to match. I remembered the doctor's warning that the old man was now blind and could not even shave. He hated beards.

He was emaciated, almost skeletal. His massive hands were all that remained recognizable of the man who was my father. I could not look on those hands without remembering all the beatings. I could see the thick fingers as my father gnawed them, often until they bled. I could see them again flipping magazine and book pages backwards, an odd habit he had, perhaps pouring through a seed catalogue while making selections for the next year's planting. I could see them raised in fists poised to rain blows on the object of his fury, so often me. Holding those hands, I compared them with my own and was horrified to see the similarity, except that mine had become bigger than his.

Finally I called him and slowly he awoke, his one eyebrow raised in mild surprise as it always had. It made me recall him falling asleep in church, snoring, then waking himself up with a blaring fart! I would always remember that blank, bemused look.

'Who's that?' he called out in alarm.

'It's Fred, Dad, your son.'

'Who?'

'Dad, it's Fred...your son.'

'Fred?'

'Yes Dad, it's me.' The realization slowly came over him and tears welled in his eyes. 'Oh my boy, you've come all the way from British Columbia? Oh no!' I reached out then and took the gnarly old hand in my own, and hugged the shockingly boney shoulders. In that moment the trip seemed worth the effort. Had father and son been alienated for so long by some simple misunderstanding? All those years lost for nothing? Thoughts raced through my mind, too complicated to sort out, but I knew that I had done what I had been compelled to do and that I was certainly not the only person who had suffered because of this now frail old man. There were so many others he had hurt badly; a string of damaged, broken lives lay in the wake of his passage. But still, he was my father, even though long ago he had chosen to ignore that fact. Now here I was, trying to make the appearance of being a good and loving son.

He complained that he was not doing well, 'Some vicious kind of flu', and grumbled that the nurses had turned down the lighting too low for him to see anything. He hated the hospital and immediately asked me to take him to British Columbia. I stopped him then and tried to explain. 'Christ,' I thought, 'I've come all this way to make things better and the first thing I do is to tell him that it's tits-up-time for him. Here I am, the angel of death! Whatever you do, don't burst out laughing.' It was a real possibility. Despite my dread of the moment, there have been times when I have broken into inappropriate laughter while extremely anxious. This was one of those moments. Or did I want to laugh vindictively? I recalled the times that this same person, my own father, had crushed me against a wall or the floor as a small boy and raged maniacally that he knew how to kill people with his bare hands and that I had better not do anything more to upset him. 'Now it's my turn, you old prick,' I thought to myself. It seemed bizarre to be outwardly calm and consoling, all the while thinking such bitter thoughts.

How often in life do we experience these moments of paradox? Saying one thing, but meaning something entirely the opposite, lying through our teeth as it is said. But then, I had been taught well. Whatever my father had claimed, promised or pronounced could never be counted on as truth or fact. He was a mythomaniac, a psychopathic liar, someone who openly espoused raw fantasy, believing it himself and expecting you to do the same. I had learned to respond in kind, at first in order to avoid his martial law then to throw him off-track about where I was living or what I was doing. That dubious skill served me through parts of my youth when I thought I had to pretend to be something or someone I was not. The only problem with consummate prevarication is that it leads to more lies. As I learned, one can completely discredit oneself. That happened to my father throughout his life. He never learned. Perhaps he was simply unable to separate reality from fantasy, but then we all, to varying degrees, spend our lives chasing illusions.

Certain that he must already know, I told him slowly and carefully that he was dying and did not have much time. He seemed to relax then, as if receiving the news for the first time, softly exclaiming, 'Well that's it for me then!' and lapsed into a long silence, staring blankly. Suddenly he said, 'I've had a good run you know, I'm a hundred years old!' He was really nearer to seventy- three. For my father, life was a weird game he played with himself. You had to tag along behind, guessing what he was really thinking. He was soon muttering again about the darkness. I patiently and repeatedly explained that he was blind. Only by holding his own hand in front of him and forcing him to reach out to it with his other, was I able to convince him that he could see nothing. He was quite annoyed about his meals. 'Good food is worth seeing,' he declared and wanted me to bring him a light, despite what he had just been told. He was quite insistent that the nurses let him wear his glasses. I realized what a horrible thing it must be to lose your sight, especially after having had it for a lifetime.

Suffering from an over-active imagination and now without vision, he was even more prone to create strange new worlds. Throughout his life, seeming at times to be schizophrenic, he had often had a difficult time with reality. Now it was hard for me to separate the effects of the tumour from his natural flaws. I pitied the staff that had to care for him and others like him in the same geriatric ward. I learned from the nurses that despite his sightlessness he was somehow able to grope the nurses whenever they came within reach of his bed. They were amazed at the accuracy of his fondling and soon learned to stay beyond range of his grasp, threatening to increase his medication if his indiscretions continued. As I arrived at the hospital each morning I inquired how he had passed the night. Often the reply was, 'Randy again'!

After a few hours at his bedside I could take no more, especially after learning upon arrival at the hospital that my father's brother and a cousin from Britain were arriving the next day. Having left England almost fifty years earlier, the old man wanted nothing to do with them. Now, I was going to have to baby sit them as well as attending to everything else. The realization of what lay ahead in the next few days was shattering.

I walked out of the hospital into a brilliant, warm afternoon. It was one of those spring days when, if you listened carefully, you believe you might be able to actually hear leaves and blossoms bursting out eagerly into the fragrant warmth. I determined to seize the moment and enjoy it as best I could. Making my way downtown to the waterfront I was soon immersed in childhood recollections. There can be no stronger stimulant to memory than the sense of smell. As I walked by the band shell in the little shoreline park, something familiar hung in the air. At first I couldn't place the odour and then realized that I stood in front of a house by the park where I had once worked as a garden boy. It hit me, fresh paint!

It was still there, that goddamned white picket fence, and still as formidable a painting project as ever. I had spent hours there raking, digging, cleaning, painting, polishing windows at the top of rickety ladders. Later, in a second-hand book store, I would once again find this same house in a book about the cherished original architecture of Oakville. I had a small part in history! Today someone was painting a tiny historic cabin in the park and it drew my attention to the band shell where uniformed bands once played on Sunday afternoons. Oakville is a British colonial town. They built a lot of churches. There seemed to be one on each street corner and on Sundays several of them played amplified recordings of bell music.

Today, a quarter of a century later, the tradition continued. It was incredible! I could not shake the sense that here time had stood still. Little had changed. As I walked the streets, more smells from my past assailed me; cigar smoke which reminded me of a family friend who had been especially benevolent to us . Then came an aroma of fresh fish and chips which, as a boy, had been something eaten only on special occasions. Someone was burning leaves, another fragrance that brought a flood of memories, both of fall and spring. I recalled working for my father in the garden, being hired out to tend to other people's yards and I remembered the lazy, almost erotic feeling that the smell of smouldering oak and maple leaves could induce on crisp autumn afternoons.

Descending from the park I walked out onto the pier where I had spent so much time alone during my youth. It didn't seem quite as long, nor as high above the water. Its edges were crumbling, but it was still the same place. I was often drawn to this pier which guarded the creek-mouth and formed the town harbour. I would spend hours sitting up on the base of the lighthouse, winter and summer, night and day, watching the marine world around me. During the summer months visiting vessels moored to the pier, tugs, fishing boats, yachts and the occasional naval vessel.

On private docks further into the harbour yachts were kept in a marina, the grandest of all being the 'Mir '. It was a huge, glistening wooden ketch that I learned sailed the open oceans. With a cream yellow hull, and flawless varnished spars, it was my ultimate fantasy. In fact, I'll confess, it still is. It would thrill me immensely to simply touch that hull, knowing it had seen distant and exotic places. Later I would learn that the name Mir means the highest point of perfection attainable by humans. As a boy I begged myself into sailing trips aboard tiny wooden racing boats called snipes. They were open plywood sloops, clumsy and slow by modern standards. Nevertheless, it was the standard sailing boat for many and made me become hopelessly addicted to the sea and to sailing. As much time was spent righting the boats and bailing out the frigid water after a capsize, as was spent actually sailing, but it was a solid foundation for intuitive seamanship.

Freighters from around the world passed a little distance offshore, plying between the Welland Canal and the steel mills in Hamilton, back and forth to Toronto and destinations beyond the mouth of the St. Lawrence River. Tugboats busily scurried to and from their assignments with an intriguing variety of tows. These fascinated me most. One of the tugs that regularly worked these waters curiously reappeared in my life almost forty years later. It was on the opposite side of the continent in a Vancouver Island harbour where I lived. Incredibly, I found work on that boat as an engineer and fulfilled a childhood fantasy as I then began a forth career, this time working on tugs.

In early autumn, a huge lake freighter would cautiously make its way into the narrow, shallow creek. It deposited a mountain of coal in a yard beneath the first bridge across the creek, keeping the entire town supplied for the winter and following year. That ship was the first harbinger of the coming winter. Word passed around town that summer must be over, the coal boat is in town!

Originally, the lighthouse was an ancient wooden clapboard structure. It was removed and replaced with a simple light on the end of a vertical pipe. The old lighthouse was reinstalled in front of the yacht club where it now stands. Lake Ontario is famous for its vicious storms, and often waves would break over the pier. I made a game of timing them and running to the end of the pier between the breaking walls of water. I would shelter behind the huge concrete base on which the lighthouse stood, terrified but thrilled as the foaming waves crashed around me. I cannot recall why I did that, perhaps a latent death-wish, but knew that being around water was, and always would be, an essential part of my life. It was a dangerous sport but not the only one I played on that lakeshore.

From the pier, during winter on calm, clear days, you could see a plume of steam from Niagara Falls rising above the broad, open horizon of the lake. When winter storms assailed the shores, you could hear the roar of surf miles inland. The pier and shoreline would be coated thickly with ice that might linger until spring. Sometimes, the lake would freeze out from the shore a tremendous distance. Old folks told of past times when the ice was so hard and thick that people skated up to a mile offshore and even went all the way to Toronto, thirty miles away. In spring, huge ice formations from the winter storms would cling to the shore, often hanging out over the water and eroding slowly from beneath. I remembered how I and a few other boys would bounce up and down on the outer edges of these ice pans until they broke off and floated in the lake. Twice we did not make it back to shore, drifting slowly out into the lake as the ice we stood on decayed visibly. We were rescued each time after someone telephoned TOWARF. This was a volunteer rescue group that called themselves the "Town of Oakville Air and Water Rescue Force". Their headquarters stood at the foot of the pier and kept a high-speed rescue launch in readiness. There was hell to pay for the boyish pranks but it did not deter us from thoughtlessly repeating the offence each year. The TOWARF building and boat still stood in the same place, evidently as ready as ever for action.

During the spring and summer, storms would deposit various layers of algae and dead fish on the beach and pier. The smelt spawned every year. Oakville's large immigrant Mediterranean population loved the little fish. Men would go onto the pier with lanterns, dip nets, camp stoves and frying pans catching and eating the tiny wriggling silver smelts. They usually fished in the darkness, each of their lanterns casting a bright pool of light into the water along the pier. They kept buckets of the odorous little fish which presumably were taken home to eat. My father also held his own special value for them. He would take me to the pier to shovel up truck-loads of dead, rotting, fetid fish to bury in his garden. His tomatoes were huge.

I walked the shingled beach for a short distance, along mounds of small flat beach stones that I once spent hours skipping on the water. Some were filled with tiny fossils and there were plenty to be found. The foreshore in places had been reinforced with old concrete slabs. I once spent hours lurking among the musty piles trying to find the perfect cave where I could hide away, sometimes stashing things toward the day when I imagined that I might actually run away and live on the beach. They were dank holes, slimy, coated with spider webs and algae, but at least they provided a token hope for refuge from the constant acrimony at home. Bitterly I thought of all the time that I had spent alone, too crippled emotionally to make enduring friendships. I was too young and frightened to escape the sorry situation I was in and over which I had no control. There seemed to be no one who cared and no hope of rescue from the horror of two angry, abusive parents. Several times as a child I contemplated suicide. If it had not been for the terrifying indoctrinations of the family's maniacal, fundamentalist religion, I would probably have leapt from a bridge. Fear of the unknown and the possibility of hellfire slightly exceeded the misery of my existence.

As I began to focus on some of these unhappy memories, it occurred to me how strange the parameters of my parents' concern were. Subjected to a harsh and violent discipline, zealous Christian doctrines, worked often like a farm animal, I did however find time for myself, usually during the periods of especially heated battles between my mother and father. Then there seemed to be no concern about where I went, whom I was with or what I was doing. It has always been so with both of them. After long periods of separation, sometimes years, they would, when reunited with one of their offspring, each invariably begin the visit with extended accounts about themselves and their problems, and showed no concern or interest for their son or daughter or grandchildren. In a meeting with my father's doctor I mentioned how peculiar it seemed that my parents shared the same bizarre personality traits. He responded that medical professionals noted that it was a common phenomenon.
'Somehow,' he said, 'They send out signals and find each other. The results are so often tragic!'

I had not thought about my childhood for years, pushing it to the furthest recesses of my memory. Now it became lodged in the front of my mind. How had I survived those years? What painful memories they held. No matter how many good things I recalled, there was a dark, lurking recollection ready to spring unexpectedly into my consciousness. I had successfully buried most of those memories for a very long time, but now they confronted me here on the beach. Knowing they would haunt me at least for the remainder of my trip, I determined to try and acknowledge only the happy memories, hopefully displacing the black experiences. However, for every joy, for every pleasant recollection, there were a dozen horrors that would not be ignored. They required an exorcism that had never been within my realm of power.

I am cursed with a crystalline memory; it is an eternal agony to be unable to forget. Unbelievably, my earliest recollection is of an event which occurred when I could have been no more than six months old. Often I wonder if these memories are merely inventions, imagined events that I have conjured up. Now at middle age it was time to confirm these memories, to confront and exorcise my demons, but for the moment, with the affairs at hand. All I could hope for was distraction and escape. Knowing what ordeals lay ahead in the next few days, I felt already near breaking point. I could not let myself dwell on any unpleasantness from the past. Unfortunately, as I would soon discover, the memories would not stop preying on me. I had suppressed them too long. Now they came rushing back. I would be forced to deal with them, and forced to summon the means to empower myself. It was to be a time of painful healing.

Leaving the shore I returned to where I had left my vehicle in the town. As I walked I revelled in the ambience of the old town. Most houses were grand, made of brick, and all were nearly two hundred years old. Each house displayed a plaque near the front entrance, indicating the date of construction and the name and occupation of the original owner: 'John Stubbert, Shipwright, 1813' or 'Henry McInnisfal, Cooper, 1849'. All the homes were lovingly maintained and, in the soft clear light of the spring afternoon, the neighbourhood was a soothing, peaceful place to be.

As a child these homes had seemed alien to me, regal, unattainable and the life-style they represented was incomprehensible fantasy. My parents had rented drab, tacky, little houses, one after another. The owners and landlords were usually peculiar characters. I was always embarrassed about the houses we lived in. When I did have friends, I could never bring them home with me. The houses were humiliating and so were my parents. They deliberately existed like backwoods bumpkins in the middle of a town filled with Presbyterian sensibilities and middle class values. I knew that we offended people. My parents were gormless and coarse. They squabbled constantly between themselves and often provoked hostilities with others including employers. They had fared poorly on all of the many farms where my father had worked as a hired hand. When we moved to town, I suffered eternal humiliation and always felt inferior, longing for the isolation of rural life. I was a misfit.

My mother dressed me in cheap, ill-fitting clothes, sometimes home-made, often garishly patched, second-hand articles purchased from thrift stores and then remade. I was constantly ridiculed and ostracized at school by the other children. For years I bore the label, 'farmer', a biting insult at the time in a North American suburb of the 1960's. Our family would go to elegant churches, arriving in an old vehicle, dressing incongruously and behaving inappropriately. It was as if being weird were a virtue. Today, I mused, we might have been considered 'cool'. Perhaps, after all, we were thirty years ahead of our time!

I spent a good part of my early adulthood desperately trying to integrate myself into the world around me, but without knowing intuitively how to fit in with the status quo; I often embarrassed myself while trying. Of course I survived all of that, went off on my own and made myself a life despite all my inhibitions and insecurities. However, I have always felt like an outsider, never belonging, never understanding. The few friends I have made, even as an adult, are similar characters. Now as I grow older I deliberately reject the average, taking pride in standing apart from a society that appears senseless to me. I have become firmly resolved to be a misfit.

Now I was able to view these homes not with envy, but a sense of superiority. I was the wronged son returning, wise and hardened to worldly ways. It occurred to me that many of these people lived sheltered little lives, and while they might be much more secure financially, I could not envy them because nothing seemed to ever change. Life appears to be nothing more than a dull ritual which these people practise while waiting to die. The streets and home were peaceful and quaint, their unchanged permanence was reassuring, but did not represent anything that I longed for. I drove away, bemused that after the initial joy of nostalgia, I did not regret having left this place behind. It was only an amusing place to visit. I felt no urge to stay.

Turning left and driving to the east, I went only a few blocks before swerving to the curb, stopped with amazement. There, absolutely unchanged, was the home of old Angus McTavish, the Scottish landlord from whom my father had rented the same property for thirty-five years. As a child, this character had always seemed old and eccentric to me. My sister and I performed clumsy acrobatics on the lawn at his bidding in exchange for the coins he flipped to us while he cackled and slapped his legs. I despise people, especially children, subjecting themselves to self-degradation for reward, simply to amuse another who is attempting to confirm their own superiority. But then, who is the more pathetic creature?

Always wearing the same black suit and fedora, Angus travelled around town husbanding his various holdings, in an ancient, gleaming black Chrysler chauffeured by his handy-man, Harvey. A quiet, gruff fellow, always attired in bib overalls, Harvey had a hunched back and a huge goitre on his throat. He smoked cigarettes compulsively, Royal Mail tobacco hand-rolled in newspaper. He possessed a mysterious quality that intrigued and terrified me all at once. Harvey would now be long dead, as was his master Angus who had finally conceded his mortality only few months previously.

The house where Angus had lived was a ramshackle, unpainted clap-board building dominating a small lot on the main street of town, sandwiched between the high brick walls of stores on either side. The house sat defiantly behind its wrought-iron fence like a last bastion of stinginess and Gaelic austerity, the foot-long grass and untamed flower beds sprawled beneath the crowning glory, a monstrous Magnolia tree. This tree, a local landmark, was today in magnificent full bloom. Old Angus had built a small empire from a monument business, but the tree was his only legacy. He had died at the age of ninety-three, unmarried, with no will and no heirs to an estate of apparently over nine-million dollars. Lucy, his 'housekeeper', now in her seventies, lived on alone in the house, apparently the closest family he had. Unfortunately there was no provision for her and the fortune was in the hands of the public trustee - as good as lost.

My father had rented a half-acre of land and an old farm house from Angus and maintained it all those years on the alleged promise that he would eventually inherit it. It was a shirtsleeve arrangement and gullibly, on one simple promise, dad had poured half of a lifetime into that dream. I suspect that the proposal existed only in my father's dreams. Possibly old McTavish had made this offer to keep a good tenant. The property was now worth a small fortune, but whatever agreement there may have been didn't matter anymore. One of them was dead and the other was following close behind.

Across the street from this house stood a brick church. Mother had taken me there a few times. The congregation was entirely black, and held rollicking musical services that were infectiously uplifting. Why my mother ever went there I could not recall, although it seemed to be a far happier church than most. There, everyone seemed to thrive on a joyful interpretation of their faith, quite unlike the doom-mongering that most fundamentalist sects embraced. At another time she discovered a small German Pentecostal congregation that met in an old house. We attended for several months although no-one there spoke a single word of English. A short, round man with a sweating, red face expostulated the terrors of Armageddon in crisp Teutonic rhetoric. I could not understand a word. Neither could my mother, but she asserted that the 'Spirit' interpreted for her. Outlandish displays of frantic Pentecostal emotion were an international language.

Mother and father moved from church to church. Something would be said or done to offend their unpredictable sensibilities and they would move on. At times, I'm sure they would be deliberately motivated to move on. Often they each went separately to a church of their own choice. Depending on the tides of domestic dispute, I would have to accompany one parent or the other to their latest church. It often meant that I would end up going to church twice on Sunday and to prayer meetings and various religious functions throughout the week. For a while my mother attended the congregation of an evangelist named Brother Ness. There was a famous night club in Mimico, near Toronto called the 'Palace Pier', built on the shore of Lake Ontario at the mouth of the Humber River. It was rented on Sunday mornings for church meetings, incongruously reeking of night-club smells from closing time only a few hours before. Sometimes empty bottles, glasses and full ash trays sat on tables that had been pushed aside for the church meeting. The 'stench of iniquity' hung like a cloud of doom over the incantations of the raving preacher who stood behind his portable pulpit on the bandstand of the club, a huge sequined curtain hanging behind him.

His sermons were a predictable rhetoric, as he had been trained in preacher academy to work a crowd with the best revenue-producing sermons. They were sickeningly similar and repetitive. Amazingly, there are still bands of frauds finding success in front of huge, mindless crowds and television audiences. Ness berated his faithful flock, working himself into a frenzied tirade about the evils of the world, and the unprepared state of mankind for the doom at hand. The imminence of Armageddon was a constant theme. The apocalypse eclipsed all horror. 'Any day, any moment now, Gabriel's trumpet will sound and you are not ready! Jesus will come like a thief in the night! God has sent me to deliver you', he screamed, leaping and gesticulating for emphasis. 'And here I am!'

The followers of these charlatans possess a sheep-like compulsion to be berated, intimidated, extorted and intimidated. The cumulative effect is for the congregation to be worked into a frenzied mob, induced to 'let the Spirit fill' them, the evidence being gibbering, twitching, drooling, leaping, finally convulsing and writhing on the floor. 'Holy Rollers' they are often called. By whatever name, they are ripe for the picking, emotionally and financially. I am somewhat demophobic and suspect that my apprehension about crowds is due in part to the evangelical madness I experienced as a child.

Oral Roberts, a popular television evangelist of the time, came to Toronto for a 'miracle and healing crusade'. He brought his huge circus tent and entourage, attracting devout hypochondriacs from a huge radius. My mother was one of them. She always had an ailment from which she beseeched God to deliver her.

I recall sitting in that audience. Even as a boy I was disgusted to see how gullible people were. They deliberately sought the embracing influence of a throng of peers wanting divine interruption in their dreary lives. People lined up to go onto the stage with the evangelist, then leapt from wheelchairs, danced waving now-useless crutches, read scripture through moments-before blind eyes, spit up invisible cancers, spoke in loud, silly voices and then coughed out demons. It was an impressive show. Swaying enraptured, arms uplifted in holy supplication, the mob eagerly filled the cardboard buckets of prowling ushers, donating their savings, their family budgets and whatever cash they carried. Exhorted to be extorted, the crowds listened to the scheming frauds tell about God blessing them for giving all they had, no matter how small, just like the widow's mite, so long as it was everything they had. God was happy with nothing less. Bastards! I cannot count the meagre meals I ate while on the cupboard sat a tiny plastic icon, a model of the 'Tower of Prayer', the evangelist's monument to himself, partially built with our grocery money. I can still hear his nasal Oklahoma drawl inviting my mother and a million other fools to put their hands on the television while he prayed for their healing. Then the address where they could send donations was repeatedly and prominently displayed. 'Send your money to Jesus! Make out the cheque to me!'

When I was very young we frequented another fundamentalist group that came together in an old one-room school house. The sermons were incessant in their theme about the 'Second Coming'. One New Year's Eve, the congregation met to celebrate the event and as the evening wore on, the minister kept hysterically referring to the end of the year. Too young to understand the difference between the end of a year and the end of the world, I became increasingly terrified as the countdown to midnight progressed. I could not comprehend why everyone around me seemed unconcerned, in fact several faces glowed with zealous anticipation. It was a terrifying experience.

Often, during fundamentalist church meetings, people

in the congregation would be requested to stand and give 'testimony' about what Jesus had done to 'save' them and alter a life where they had been 'lost in sin'. It was predictable rhetoric and often men would claim that they did not 'drink anymore'. I wondered that they must be very thirsty and could not understand what was virtuous about a parched throat. When one of these people once came for dinner, I carefully observed that the man drank water, milk, and tea. I was left even more confused. 'Little people are best seen and not heard' was the stock reply whenever I dared raise a question and so I was left to muddle it out on my own as usual. 'Christ', I mused aloud to myself as I pulled out into the traffic and drove away, 'No wonder I'm so damned screwed up'.

Two blocks further down the street I recognized the Dairy Freeze, a landmark drive-in hamburger stand that was still doing business in the same location after several decades. It was an icon of the fifties and all the wild and wonderful things that my parents abhorred. Young people in cars, rock'n roll, booze, cigarettes which naturally led to marijuana and then heroin addiction, short skirts, long slicked-back hair, drive-in movies, which inevitably lead to illegitimate pregnancy and insidious venereal disease - all were devices of Satan to corrupt lives and enslave souls. Anything that repulsed the fundamentalists mesmerized me with longing. A description of some evil made me tingle with desire for it. Now people stood in line patiently waiting to order their deadly junk food in defiance of the golden arches that had risen less than half a block away. It was a refreshing sight. What was once a symbol of rebellion had become a bastion of tradition.

A short distance further along I came upon my old high school, looking exactly the same, except that it was now a Catholic school with a new name. What memories here! The graveyard across the road was where classmates and I had gone to smoke cigarettes while we lounged against the headstones talking about girls and cars, making plans for after school and the coming weekend. I supported myself while in high school, working steadily when not in class, and was seldom able to indulge in social activities with my peers. I always lived on the fringes, ostracizing myself out of necessity and insecurity, believing that I was not able to fit and then afraid that I might. This cemetery was the same place where my father had once dug graves for a living, building bonfires to thaw the frozen ground. It was the first winter after we had moved to town. He would come home cold and exhausted, but would be gone again into the winter night to drive taxi so he could earn a few extra dollars until he found a proper job.

I surveyed the school grounds, even remembering specific trees and events that had occurred near them. There was a flood of faces and names. In 1965, the year that I first came to this school, I also left home at the age of fourteen. It was a few weeks after my mother had taken my sister and left the house, moving to British Columbia. I had essentially begun to live a double life. I held several small jobs to survive. Fortunately I was big and could lie about my age. I stayed in boarding houses; bed and breakfast was then ten dollars per week. Sometimes I drifted back home, but it never worked out. I was clearly a nuisance to my father and there were often violent fights. I did not want anyone else to know my situation, and I asked for no sympathy. I had to do everything on my own, and I was determined to graduate. I did, with a scholarship. I have been fiercely independent the rest of my life often at great personal expense, especially without the basic guidance that I needed during those formative years in regard to financial and social skills. But then, neither of my parents had possessed these skills to pass on to me.

Fondly I recalled teachers who had given me special attention and extra help, perhaps knowing more about my personal life than I understood. It was only after I met my wife, ironically also a school teacher, that I considered their extra efforts and often wished I could thank them for their support. Now I stood in front of the school that I had left twenty-eight years earlier. I thought of some of my class-mates and wondered what had become of them. During my entire visit to Oakville, I found myself looking at everyone I passed and met, hoping to see a familiar face. There were none, other than one woman. We met in a crowded hallway and exchanged a brief, reciprocal flicker of vague recognition before we were swept off in opposite directions. I stood by the school, remembering those events and feelings as if they were yesterday. Yet they seemed so far away, only a distant and improbable imagining. What had been real?

My eyes blurred as I realized that there had been little chance to be either a child or a teenager. I drove on musing that there can be nothing more thoughtless to steal than someone's childhood. That pilferage occurs not only in third world countries out of economic necessity. Tragically, it occurs increasingly in our contemporary western society where children so often seem bereft of their innocence and have no instinct for discovery. They feel they have seen it all on television or the internet, our modern electronic babysitters. There is no more tragic figure than a cynical child with no sense of wonder or trust.

Soon I passed Appleby College, a private school for boys. It was traditionally British. Typical of private schools all around the world, there were uniforms for the students. The boys all wore grey flannel shorts, knee socks, wool vests and little green caps. They never went anywhere alone and were often seen walking in groups along the highway. No-one was in sight as I drove past that day but nothing appeared to have changed in over a quarter-century. Next to the school was the Cedar Croft Motor Hotel, also apparently unchanged. I decided to turn in there and rent one of the cabins arranged around the long circular, gravel driveway. Remarking to the proprietor that this motel looked the same as it had when I was a child, I learned that the business had been open for seventy-two years. On presenting my visa card I was told that only cash was accepted, one of the things that hadn't changed here since the twenties!

When this region of Southern Ontario was originally colonized by the British, it was surveyed methodically and pragmatically. Data were established that were noted as county or town lines and ran due north from the lakeshore. From these points of reference, more lines were established at one mile intervals, some of which eventually became roads. The streams that ran into the lake were even described by their distance from a datum. Now I turned north onto the Fourth Line, a road where I'd lived when I was three years old.

At that time my father had been an orchard-keeper for a sophisticated elderly Englishman who owned an estate known as Winton Farms. I crossed a bridge over the stream where my father had once picked watercress and caught snapping turtles. I remembered one in a bushel basket that he taunted with an old broom handle. It promptly snapped the stick in two with its jaws and I was warned to stay away from the creek. That was his way; there was always a hidden terror or threat to consider.

Now I cast my eyes on the manor house. It seemed faded and far smaller than the castle-like grandeur that I had held in my memory. Beside the house, however, was the well, exactly the same as I recalled. It had a round field-stone base and a shingle roof over the windlass. I was sternly admonished to stay away from the well for fear I fall in. Behind the well and the house stood the barn where apples were stored, and the sheds that housed the truck and tractors. Once a week my mother and father took the farm vehicle, an old Ford single-axle dump truck, to town on business and to do our shopping. I could still hear the whine of the gears and recall the rich truck smell.

Once my mother had completed her shopping at the Loblaws grocery store, we would wait in a lakeside park for my father to complete the farm's business and meet us. Often in summer we would slice up a watermelon and eat it while we waited. Mother had worked as a part-time maid in the big house and assisted another woman named Clara, who was the cook and managed the house-keeping. She was especially notable to me because I had been told she had a glass eye. Whenever I was near her I would try to determine which eye was the artificial one. Old man Parker as he was known, the lord of the manor, often went for walks along the Fourth Line with his two white Scottish terriers. Mrs. Parker held them on long leashes and the old man had a walking stick that he twirled jauntily between steps.

At the north end of the orchards were several cabins, referred to as 'pickers' cottages'. These were only occupied during harvest and my parents moved into the largest one which was closest to the road. It was a place where strong memories were forged and many formative events occurred. I drove slowly up the road toward that site, knowing the old shack was long-gone. My memories were confirmed as I noted the remains of the orchard, now only visible as random apple trees on the lawns of suburban homes, which themselves were obviously long standing. A sense of oldness washed over me. I drove past a house where a young friend had lived opposite us. That house fixed the location of one of my former homes over forty years ago. A row of pine trees along the road marked the precise location, the biggest one with a thick horizontal branch was where I had once sat in a rope swing, wearing a little red straw cowboy hat. Later I would discover an old photograph of that swing and my friend and I riding on it.

I recalled happy visits from a favourite aunt, who always brought toys and treats. Often they were things like alarm clocks and tin aeroplanes which I usually managed to take apart but could seldom re-assemble in working order. While we lived here, mother had taken me to her birthplace on a homestead in northern Saskatchewan and, all these years later, some details of that trip were still vivid. We had returned to this small home with my grandfather, someone who looked much like the old man in the painting 'American Gothic'. He was a stern unsmiling man, impatient with small children like me. I can recall no special moments between us.

We had travelled to 'the homestead', as my mother always referred to the family farm, on what was one of the last steam-powered Canadian transcontinental passenger trains. The route through northern Ontario wove its curving way around a million lakes and I could see the engine far ahead belching black smoke and billowing steam, its massive connecting rods rhythmically rising and falling to the revolutions of the huge, spinning, steel-spoked wheels. Misunderstanding the railway schedule, my mother had taken me for a walk when the train finally stopped in Winnipeg. We stood on a bridge over the Red River admiring a westbound passenger train as it pulled out of the station. We later realized that we had been admiring our own train. It was a fortuitous error. The train had later derailed, with some passengers killed and injured. Family members waiting for our arrival were grief-stricken when we could not be accounted for. Unaware, we spent a long night trying to rest on hard oak benches in the huge echoing railway station under the glare of bright lights and schedule announcements. This was an era when the nation still travelled extensively by train and the station never slept. In later years I spent many sleepless nights in train stations as I wandered the country on my own, too broke to rent lodgings, the weather too severe to be outside.

The next day my mother made sure we were on the following train, loudly giggling to everyone aboard about her funny story of watching our own train leave the previous day. It was only when we arrived at our destination that we learned of the previous day's train accident. We sat in the dining car for lunch while the train was coupled to a new locomotive. A large jolt splashed a bowl of scalding hot tomato soup on the shirt of another young boy in the car. I remember that the screaming child wore a white and red-striped T shirt, the same sort of shirt worn by a cartoon character that advertised Campbell's tomato soup. It was odd, I mused, how the vagaries of memory worked. There are so many things I would just as soon forget and others that I wish I could recall more clearly. Occasionally something that seemed to be a perfectly accurate recollection proves to be raw fabrication: some days, one is hard-pressed to recall what one had for breakfast.

Finally we arrived at the station in Kindersley. It was a cold, bleak afternoon; mother was indignant that no-one was there to meet us. The waiting room was open and we sat there out of the keening wind, waiting. I can still recall the sense of that lonely place, that desolate emptiness of northern Saskatchewan, of being hungry, cold, afraid and unnerved by mother's incessant complaining. I vaguely recall her tittering maniacally as I peed into a black coal-pail that sat beside the coal box in the waiting room; she would not let me go outside into the blowing cold. It was a convenient urinal for me but how valuable is a bucket full of piss- wet coal? A large pot-bellied stove sat silent and cold in the middle of the waiting room. It was up to waiting passengers to keep the stove going. It must have been sometime in October when we arrived. The grass, tall and dry, rattled in the incessant prairie wind. I remember how it stood slightly higher than my three-year-old eye level and the intimidating mystery of what lay beyond in the trackless, surging expanses.

For a while we stayed with a bachelor uncle and his big dog in a large, unfinished frame house that stood far out and alone on the undulating prairie. I have observed that it was a family tradition, or perhaps a prairie custom, to erect buildings to a certain point of usability and then progress no more toward completion. Many people who lived on the prairie during the great depression of the 1930s survived in impromptu shelters, minimally adequate against the elements. Aesthetics were an abstract consideration. Paint, floor coverings, inner wall finishing, plumbing, landscaping – all were decadence beyond consideration. Wherever mother's siblings moved and acquired property, they would erect a crude, ramshackle building. Then, instead of completing and tidying that project, another building and yet another would be thrown up in the same manner until their land was filled with rickety fire-hazards. An ensuing stage would be to fill each construction with every possible kind of junk; 'It might come in handy some day'. It was often hard to discern a residence from a storage building, a stable or chicken coop.

As my uncles aged they sold their holdings, usually at a discounted price. The accumulated debris had to be cleared away by the truckload. Who knew what to do with collapsing sheds filled, and often held erect, with used and forgotten stove-pipes, expired furnaces, cook stoves, water heaters, refrigerators, mouldy ancient magazines, cans of used nails, discarded bottles, broken tools, old toilets and mysterious collections of no worth even to a scrap dealer? The labour of sorting it all out far exceeded any latent value. A quirk of some people who have known hard times is to hoard as much material as possible. Their packrat philosophy is that a mountain of any sort of goods represents a tangible evidence of well-being. They prefer a yard full of crude huts to the elegance of one, properly finished building, or a collection of derelict vehicles and parts to a single, dependable conveyance.

There is an anecdote about an elderly farmer who retires to town and slowly adjusts to the luxury of running water and going to the bathroom *inside* the house. One morning, while completing his ablutions, as he pulled up his coveralls a dime fell from his pocket into the toilet. He pondered the situation, not wanting to stick his hand into the mess. Finally digging into the depths of his pocket, he extracts a quarter and throws it in as well! Reaching into the loaded toilet for ten cents was one matter, thirty-five was an entirely new situation. My mother's family thought a lot like that.

At night in my uncle's house, mother and I slept in a bed near a woodstove. I remembered lying awake in the dark listening to the wind moan and shift the creaking building. Drafts found their way into the house, cold and swirling, whistling shrilly in sudden bursts. Outside, coyotes yelped and wailed as light from the stove's mica door danced across the ceiling in ominous, flitting shapes. The coyotes terrified me. They came close to the unfenced house, finding cover in the long grass which towered above my height. Visiting the outhouse was a gauntlet for me with those curious wild beasts lurking nearby. Once, as a prank, my uncle had hidden in the grass and imitated their calls. The beasts responded and began circling nearer, singing their blood-curdling coyote song all the while. Horrified by their advance, I sequestered myself in the privy. In that outhouse a box sat filled with old school books in lieu of toilet paper. I loved these books; too young yet to read, I enjoyed the drawings and invented stories to suit. During that visit, if I became bored, it was likely that I had run the coyote gauntlet to pour through the outhouse library, oblivious to its malodorous ambience.

We visited another uncle, first meeting him in town.

At the far end of the broad, gravel main street, my mother pointed him out at work high atop a bright red grain elevator where he was repairing the roof. In later years he would fall from a similar place. He lived, but his health faltered for the rest of his life. His house was a dark shack in the bottom of a shallow gully. It reeked of kerosene and the bed that I was sent to was unmade. The cold sheets were twisted and grey, rifle shells and pocket change were littered beneath the stinking blankets. Obviously the man slept on the dirty bed fully clothed. Outside this place, pathetic, dung-caked cattle milled about forlornly in a muddy enclosure. Their sporadic bawling continued through the night. In the distance, smouldering piles of roots and trees flamed and flickered in the night, their combined acrid smoke settling in the night air like fog. The poplar and spruce forests of Northern Saskatchewan were being cleared and burned for farmland; the acrid pyres provided an ominous atmosphere to the landscape.

Even at the age of three, I had felt a thrill of discovery about travelling, but it was mixed with a sense of dread about this alien place. In the following days there were visits to some of mother's girlhood haunts. There was a day at a wild cranberry bog where I entertained myself by making noises that echoed repeatedly across the water from the surrounding dark, silent forest. My sounds were punctuated only by the hoarse calls of ravens. In other areas the incessant wind rattled golden, shimmering leaves in endless forests of poplar trees. Beneath their shivering branches, an aromatic carpet of the fallen leaves lay in all directions. These trees often grow in the advance of a forest reclaiming land taken and cleared from it by man or natural cataclysm. They are often found on abandoned farms where they crowd around and invade derelict buildings, accelerating the decay of the structures which lean and then collapse before the onslaught of the elements. In that region, despite the ongoing destruction of the forests to create more farmland, at that time many homesteads had been forsaken as failures and were turning again into the forests from which they had so arduously been carved. Whenever I smell that cloying tang of autumnal leaves, I am overcome with a sad, lonely heaviness.

On another occasion we visited my mother's old one-room schoolhouse at a place called Miner's Creek. She had spend parts of several years there, but never progressed beyond the third grade. Most of my uncles had little better than grade one or two schooling, drifting off to menial jobs at a tender age to help support the family or make their own way. They all did poorly in school. I am sure that was due in part to an inadequate diet and the long distance they walked even in the bitter cold of winter. They have stories of taking turns going to school on alternate days, too few pairs of winter boots shared between them. Their truancy was probably due to my grandfather's apathy toward their education. By all accounts they were left to their own devices and choices. For a child, sitting in a one-room school would have seemed irrelevant to the business of raising cattle and crops. The school was no longer used but the door was unlocked. All the books were still on the shelves, chalk sat on the ledges beneath the blackboards, the windows and the woodstove were intact. I recall that there was no vandalism and that my mother and her brothers regarded the school as a sort of edifice. They often spoke of their school and teacher with reverence, and remembered the place with a regretful nostalgia, wishing sadly that they had then understood the value of a basic education.

We went to stay at the 'homestead'. My grandparent's home was a pathetic tarpaper shack where they had raised the nine children who had survived birth. There was no electricity and water was packed in buckets from a muddy stream that ran behind a decrepit barn. A wood heater stood in the middle of the floor. I vaguely recollect a horrible fight one night when my enraged mother had chased a brother around that stove again and again, slashing at him with a hatchet. The dispute ended only when she had exhausted herself, its origins most likely an insignificant event long in the past. To this day the entire family has an enormous capacity for harbouring grudges. Two brothers who lived within a stone's throw of each other never spoke to each other for over seventeen years, both waiting for the other to apologize after an argument about a garden rake. They are both dead now; so far as anyone knows they never reconciled.

Gormlessness was bred into all of them. By all accounts my grandfather was a strange character with an irrational constitution of rights and wrongs. Devoutly religious, he insisted on nightly scripture readings despite poor eyesight and the lack of lamp oil. There are incredulous stories of systematically burning wood shavings for light enough to read the massive family bible. A sleigh-load of firewood would be laboriously cut, split and hauled into a bakery in town where it was bartered for a sack of flour. Cows starved in the barnyard while the family existed on turnips and biscuits. Deer roamed in abundance throughout the surrounding countryside, but it was forbidden to eat unclean meat. Despite the hunger and privation of the large family, there are accounts of the children huddling together in too-few beds within their tiny home, listening while their father demanded and exercised nightly conjugal rights. My grandmother was in her mid forties when she gave birth to the last of her children.

During our stay there winter descended with a sudden fury. One morning we awoke to discover that one of grandma's numerous cats had become caught between an inner and outer window. I t had frozen solid during the night. Despite the cats, the place was infested with vermin. One night a rat bit my sleeping grandfather in the middle of his bald head. I recall a weasel in a winter coat of ermine white that regularly popped through a small hole in the floor. I made a game of placing a bottle cap over the hole and watching the creature lift the cap on its head when it came up through the hole. 'Pop goes the weasel', I cried delightedly, much to the amusement of everyone.

It snowed one night and throughout the following day. The storm exhausted itself near sundown and everyone went outside into the clear twilight. The grass, taller than my young height, was beaten flat under the weight of whiteness which now lay even higher than the grass had stood. The air was crisp and clear, filled with the wonderful fresh, clean smell of new snow. In the distance we heard a faint, resonant snarl that grew louder by the moment. Seconds later it rose to a throaty bellow and just above the tree-tops an aeroplane appeared. It raced toward us only a hundred feet above the ground, red and green navigation lights glowing softly at either end of its bulky silhouette in the dusk. Skis were mounted on the unmistakable wide-stance undercarriage of a yellow Nordyn Norseman bush plane. It passed just in front of us while everyone stood riveted in the clearing in front of the house. The pilot rocked the wings. This is my earliest memory of an aeroplane. Those few seconds formed an indelible image that will stay with me the rest of my life. This incident probably motivated me later to start a career in aviation. As the throbbing rattle of its exhaust faded again in the gathering darkness, someone speculated that, 'It must be on a mercy flight to be out on in weather like this'.

Travel was now accomplished by horse and sleigh. There was a journey to a neighbouring farm sitting in a wagon converted onto its winter runners. I sat on the front seat next to my grandfather, swaddled in blankets as our team of horses trotted ahead of the sleigh. He loved his horses and urged them on affectionately, calling out to them by name. Their breath steamed in the frigid air and the harness jingled rhythmically. That is the one pleasant memory I have of being with that man. Years later when he lay dying, drifting in and out of lucidity, someone asked him if he knew where he was. 'Yes', he replied with certainty, 'I'm on my way to Tisdale with a sleigh-load of wood'. I understand.

Some people had fully enclosed sleighs, equipped with wood stoves and windows like a cabin on skis. The reins were led inside through little holes beneath a small, glass windshield. A single side door provided access to what must have been a top-heavy and dangerous conveyance. There was a story about one overturning in a ditch, its occupants getting horribly burned in the fire started by the sleigh's stove. On the day we went to the train station to go home, we rode in a toboggan which was a simple wooden trough dragged behind a horse. It was bitterly cold, and I remember being slammed over the frozen ruts all the way to town. My grandfather, who travelled to Ontario with us, was excited about the 'newfangled' diesel locomotive that pulled our train. I have no other memories of him and none of my grandmother.

In that little house on the Fourth Line I had a bedroom facing north toward the railway tracks. I still possess images of trains racing through the night, their whistles blowing in the distance, then nearer for each level-crossing, and finally receding again into the darkness. Sometimes I could not sleep for hours and would stand on my little bed by the window watching for them. They passed in billowing clouds of steam and smoke, the soon to be vanished trademark of these very last steam locomotives which pulled the local freight trains. Diesel powered passenger trains would trumpet by, the cars illuminated inside. I could often see passengers sitting by the windows. The pervasive throb of the sleek engines was impressive, but the era of steam power could not be surpassed for drama and splendour. There was nothing like the clank and chuffing bark of a speeding steam locomotive, or the mournful howl of the whistle, especially on a moonlit night when its huge plume of steam and smoke billowed in the night sky.

Sometimes just the singing of the crickets provided a magical symphony that kept me awake and peering into the night outside that window. The grandest memory of that place which I hold dearly always began with a low, distant, faint pulsing hum. Slowly it grew in intensity, louder and louder until it became a throbbing roar of aircraft engines and slightly unsynchronized propellers. Aircraft descended over our fields to land at Malton Airport, less than thirty miles away. They passed low over the house on their approach. Even at the age of three I make a game of identifying the aircraft by their sound before they come into sight. I knew them all: DC3s, DC4s, Northstars, Constellations, Electras and the RCAF Harvard Trainers, which often flew over in squadrons, night and day. Each type of aircraft has its own special sound. The Northstars were especially vivid because, as they passed in the night, hot, cherry red exhaust manifolds belched a jet of yellow and blue flame. The four Rolls Royce Merlin engines sang a throaty, exotic tune which anyone who has heard can never forget. Perhaps there would be a momentary gleam of reflected moonlight and a dull glow from behind oval cabin windows. Navigation lights on each wingtip alternately blinked green then red, flashing beacons reflecting their red light on the polished belly of the fuselage. Then a white tail light glowed dimmer as the airliner passed out of sight, its thundering engines fading, pulsing and mingling again into the other sounds of the night, until again there was only the song of crickets.

It was overwhelmingly magical. I was mesmerized by the aircraft. I would blink one eye and then the other to show bemused adults my imitation of the wing lights, running in circles with arms outstretched, trying to copy the drone of the engines. In those years a passing airplane would attract everyone's momentary interest. Children were always fascinated, rooted to the ground until the craft disappeared from sight. Today, efficient, near-silent jets whisper overhead, unnoticed as they proceed on non-stop flights halfway around the planet. Our accelerating technological progress is taken for granted. Now it seems to take a lot to fascinate a modern child.

I was to find that, like everywhere else, there were other, darker memories of this place. Shattering crockery, breaking furniture, slamming doors, screaming and sobbing throughout long nights, beatings indicated yet another fight between my mother and father. An indelible image is etched in my brain of a broken bowel of sugar lying on the floor, its spilled white contents slowly soaking up a pool of thick red blood. I was the pawn in their infernal game. Yet, for all the while they lived together, I was accused of being the cause of their discord. Once my father produced the ashes and burned buckle of his large belt from the firebox of the wood cook stove. I would have been three at the time. He used to 'spank' me with this belt, and that day he accused me of spitefully burning it. I had not, but I should have. I can still feel the crushing impact of the heavy buckle when dad, in an uncontrolled rage, flayed and whipped me with it for some misdemeanour, real or imagined. In fact, I was certain that my father was responsible for burning the belt. When I suggested this, I was again beaten angrily. He found a new belt.

My mother did not administer spankings or beatings, those were dad's specialty. Instead, mom held an expertise with furniture, small appliances and whatever came to hand to be thrown, be it a shoe, a shattered chair-leg, a knife, a brick or a plate. To this day I have a phobia of anyone standing behind my peripheral vision. I was always braced for the next assault. She preserved fruit and vegetables, keeping them in her "Back kitchen", an unheated room at the rear of the house. Once she had found a large garden snake there and summarily chopped it into pieces with a shovel. To her fundamentalist mind, snakes represented the epitome of evil, and she furiously performed her righteous duty. Each dying piece had wriggled off in its own direction and the snake's blood stained the wooden floor permanently. For years I had elaborate nightmares about those writhing snake parts.

The family acquired a well used but gleaming late-thirties model Ford sedan. It was worn out mechanically, but cars of that vintage did not rust and it was a beautiful black car with red wheels, chrome hubcaps and grill, huge pod headlights and shiny V8 logos on the louvered engine hood. The smell of that car's interior was magnificent, a heady mixture of upholstery and gasoline. I remember riding in it through apple orchards in full, fragrant bloom. Now as an adult I ache that the car had tragically gone to the auto-wreckers for lack of money for proper repairs. The battery was weak. Each Sunday morning as we started out for church, I would sit in the back seat while my parents, dressed in their Sunday best would push the car down a small hill behind our house. It was one of the few things I recall them doing in harmony. With both pushing mightily, the car would begin to move and my mother clambered aboard. Dad would then jump up on the running board, holding the door open with one hand, steering with the other and pumping the ground with his remaining leg. At the fateful moment of maximum speed he would leap behind the wheel and engage the clutch. If the car started, and it usually did, the battery held enough charge for the rest of the day to start the car as intended. If not, I recall the altercations when my parents had to tow it with the farm tractor. Everything could be made into an ordeal. On mornings when the car would not start, we were prevented from going to church. To my profuse and secret joy, we would trudge back to our home to listen to church programs on the radio. Eventually I could shed my tie and Sunday best clothes, and go outside to play quietly.

The tantrums, the beatings, the fights and all the happy memories of that place now blended into a bitter-sweet fog. I drove away, amazed at the clarity of my childhood memories and how easily they had been revived, each recollection spawning yet another.

A short distance to the north, past that railway crossing I remembered so well, the fourth line crossed over the QEW, the original freeway connector between Toronto and Hamilton. I was appalled at what I saw; the area was now completely changed. I had often come this way throughout my youth to go to a local cow pasture airfield. It was a private farm shared with local light-aircraft owners. The airfield and the town's harbour had been my twin Mecca. Now all was subdivisions, malls and industrial parks. Memories of that airfield had been with me ever since I'd left this place so long ago and nothing else matched their clarity. I had dreamed of returning to find it unchanged and was shattered to discover that it was gone. A final pilgrimage was impossible.

The tiny airstrip had been located atop a south-facing bluff. A winding dirt road climbed up to a large house at the corner of the field where the owner lived, a well-known local businessman. He owned a brand new amphibious Cessna but shared the field with other aircraft owners. A DeHavilland Tiger Moth and also a DeHavilland Auster were tied there. Someone else owned a Harvard. There were a few Globe Swifts, a Luscombe 8E, a Piper J3, a Vagabond, a Cessna 180 and two homebuilt airplanes. One bore the exotic name of Ganangobie and the other was a Volmer Sportsman, an unwieldy amphibian powered with a Volkswagen engine. These exotic names meant nothing to people who are not interested in aviation but they are still music to my ears. The place had been heaven to me. As I drove by the location I marvelled about how far I had repeatedly walked or cycled as a young boy to this location several miles from town.

Many times when I arrived there, the airfield was deserted. I would sit for hours beneath the fluttering, creaking windsock, content to be close to the various aircraft and my boyish fantasies. Other days there would be someone tinkering with their airplane and perhaps they were about to go flying. All my expectancy and patience might pay off. I was a sort of mascot, an airfield rat who would do anything for the hope of a ride. I mowed grass, pumped tires, washed the planes, helped change oil, and did everything possible to try and win the favour of a seat. My first airplane ride ever was here in the Luscombe. The owner took me for a ride and within minutes of that first thrill of leaving the ground, I badgered him into two loops, a roll and then a turn at the controls myself. It was everything I had dreamed of, all that I thought flight was. That day I became hopelessly addicted to flying for the rest of my life. I still hold a fascination for flight in small aircraft.

Now the airfield was gone. Only faceless suburbia lay in all directions, the traffic on the freeway hurtling past from one oblivion to another. I sat in my vehicle pondering those magnificent memories. Soaring up so long ago out of the now-vanished field over that same bluff into the turbulent lakeshore wind, rising into the clear smooth air aloft, steep wheeling turns through majestic corridors between the clouds, my tortured life became a beautiful and definable spectacle below, where the world, for those few minutes, made sense. Then there was the gliding and side-slipping back down to the bumpy, rutted pasture, and the delightful moment of suspense each time the wings transferred their burden back to the hardness of the unforgiving earth. My temporary freedom and detachment from life below was a release that kept me endowed with a stoic motivation to endure my dreary lot at home. Aviation was my dream fulfilled.

At that time I attributed a god-like quality to pilots. To me, they possessed a magical quality and courageous daring which enabled them to coax machines into the sky. A pinnacle of my life came years later when I first flew an aircraft entirely alone. As I ascended on my first solo flight, I joined the deities of my childhood. The joyful whoop of the moment will echo forever along the halls of my memory. That mystique is largely gone now; flight is commonplace, merely another way to commute as rapidly as possible. People hold no reverence for the aviator as they once did, or perhaps my fascination has become tarnished. However, at this moment it was those glorious smells that I most longed for. Just once more I wanted to breath in the heady mixed perfume of fresh-mown grass, cow manure, aviation gasoline, leather upholstery and the occasional waft of fresh fabric dope. It was bliss. A fragrance that should have been bottled, the label: 'Flight'.

Again I stood up to a brass-edged wooden propeller, pulling hard and sharp, stepping back to safety. It flickers into a smooth blur. A puff of smoke flies from the suddenly blatant exhaust. Fabric-covered wings shake themselves awake with a rattling shudder, grass flailing behind in the propeller blast as I pull the chocks away from the wheels. Finally comes the moment of commitment as the throttle is advanced, the tail rising as the rudder comes to life, biting for control into the accelerating slipstream, thumps of the rutted field coming faster, lighter, as eager wings claim our weight from the wheels. Then flight! Exultant freedom, knife-edge decisions, soaring away, no turning back, I rise beyond my earthly limit. Magic!

Lost forever now, jewel in the crown of thistles and shit that was my childhood. Sadly, wearily, I checked the time, shifted the car into gear and drove back toward town. Now it all seemed very long ago. I had so much to do yet today. The magic faded.

Chapter 2

A Bitter Pill Called Memory

I drove back into town over the Rebecca Street Bridge, which had been built soon after we first moved to town. The new bridge, smelling of fresh concrete, had seemed immense and giddily high above the creek below. Decades later it now appeared as if it had stood forever. I had often stood on that bridge, usually alone in the night, looking down at the muddy water below, sometimes contemplating the ease of a simple jump beyond the railing. It is a terrible thing for a child to regularly consider suicide. I know that now. I had never actually tried, but the damned idea always lurked there. Often, each of my parents threatened to kill themselves in an expression of despair. I had naturally assimilated the idea. Only when I reached the age of forty and the family doctor had diagnosed my ongoing fatigue and depression, did I finally understand that it is not normal to regularly contemplate suicide. The process of separating out nurture versus nature continues. The solution of suicide as a response to emotional crisis is now able to be placed on a high shelf in my head, but never in my heart. It remains an ultimate option for escape from the despair of hopelessness, of intense self-denigration, and the darkness of loneliness. Like a sinister lottery ticket, I retain the option as an ultimate escape, and there is a bizarre comfort in that.

Just around the corner I drove onto Church Street and found a parking lot. I pulled in and stopped again. Across the street from me stood a building which I knew had been the old fire hall. It was in the place we had lived for a few months. My parents, hoping for a better life and a fresh start, gave up farming and settled in town for the first time. This parking lot was the place where they had rented an upstairs apartment in an old brick building. It was reached by climbing an echoing wooden staircase. We shared a bathroom down the hall with another apartment and there was a thrift shop on the lower floor. I could remember mother clambering out through a back window to hang laundry on a line above the alley below. She was pregnant at the time and became quite ill when the shop below was renovated and painted. She was often hysterical and complained so much about everything that nobody paid much attention to her.

An aunt occasionally came to visit us there. She was the evil older sister, at least by mother's fundamentalist standards, because she wore lipstick, drank and smoked. She always brought me an interesting new toy and had once taken me to a drive-in theatre to see a cartoon and a child's movie. There was a fight later between my mother and her sister because I had been 'corrupted'. According to mother's dogma, movies were one of the many roots of evil. Other deadly snares were drinking, smoking, rock music, and night clubs. Everything led to fornication and damnation. I recall hearing her screech at my aunt: 'Next thing you're going to have him smoking cigarettes'. I was four years old.

Although the details are unclear, it was while we lived here that mother had been committed to a mental hospital in Hamilton. Her condition was described as a 'nervous breakdown'. For the rest of her life she claimed that my father and the family physician had collaborated, and that there was nothing wrong with her. Even so, she would be sent to the same hospital a second time and to other mental health facilities later in her life. Horribly, she had been given electric shock treatments during her pregnancy. It seems barbaric. I speculate that my sister's faltering health may be due in part to her hard life as a foetus. It would not get easier once she was born. Dad went to see mother on Sunday afternoons. I sat outside the ivy-covered walls and waited in a car we borrowed for the visits. Piercing dark eyes set in pallid, silent faces would stare down from behind small, barred windows. The entire place had a dark feeling about it, even on a sunny summer afternoon.

There were other memories about my summer in that apartment, the first time I lived alone with my father. I had a little white sailor suit and a plastic pirate ship that my aunt had brought me. A navy vessel arrived in the harbour one day. My father dressed me in my suit and took me to the pier to see the ship. I was photographed with some of the ship's crew and the picture appeared in a local newspaper. As a diversion during my visit, I researched the local library archives, sifting through several drawers of micro-filmed newspapers from that era but I could not find the photo.

My father enjoyed wrestling with me at times, but his game often evolved to holding me down and tickling me mercilessly. It is a horrible torture. I cannot abide seeing anyone impose themselves on another person who is trapped. I become instantly and irrepressibly angry whenever I perceive someone being a bully. My sudden missionary urge in these moments has led me into avoidable conflict more than once, but I cannot remain passive when someone, especially a child, is being victimized physically or verbally.

Desperately, I fought back against my father and once accidentally punched him in the groin. He dropped to the floor in sudden agony and after recovering, despite my obvious dread, he angrily beat me. I cowered in the sooty fireplace, terrified, hopelessly trapped, in deep pain from my father's sudden, furious blows and my frustration at his refusal to see his pain as an accident he had provoked. How often have I wondered if my father ever reflected on his rages and violence, if he ever grieved for the contempt he had shown his own children and therefore himself. I think not.

The fire hall stood across the street. I was always startled and thrilled by the rising skull-splitting moan of the station siren. I would rush to the front window to look down on the action that often happened in the night. The doors on the hall would rise as the lights blinked on.

Firemen resting in their upstairs quarters would slide down a polished brass pole, glide into their waiting boots and yellow suits,
leap into the gleaming red trucks and wail away into the darkness with lights flashing. There was a crewman who regularly chased down the street after his departing engine as he struggled into his coat. I never befriended the fire crews although they were always there, cleaning and polishing. I was forbidden to cross the street.

A birthday present I had received and owned for many years was a wooden wagon. It bore the name Werlich, painted in large red letters on the side. It had removable racks and I travelled the sidewalks by kneeling in the wagon and propelling myself along with the other foot. I steered with the tongue of the wagon folded back like the tiller of a sailboat. My left shoe was always worn out long before the other, something that took my mother a long time to comprehend. The apartment was one block above the main street and I would travel continuously around that block for hours. A corner store on the main street paid two cents apiece for returned pop bottles. I was always on patrol for them and promptly exchanged any I found for candy. My favourites were black liquorice pipes and cigars with red candy embers on the end. I would scoot off in the wagon, cigar in my mouth slowly savouring the rich flavour, my face slowly blackening with the sweet mess.

One day I swerved my wagon around a pedestrian and rammed a parking meter. The impact jarred the side of the meter loose and it hinged open. A gleaming cascade of pennies and nickels poured directly into the wagon with a loud rattle, a sum incomprehensible to me, but clearly a windfall not to be wasted. Afraid I had committed some dire criminal act, I fled with my cargo of bullion, bound directly for the corner store. My haul must have been nearly five dollars, a fortune for any young boy at that time. I returned home with my wagon heaped with every sort of candy and still had more than a dollar in change. My mother was amazed and I proudly explained how I had come by my wealth. After that I made a point of regularly ramming every meter around the block, furtively looking out for anyone who might catch me but never again was I to have similar good luck. My father could not understand why the wagon began to persistently need repairs.

During the first occasion that mother was in the hospital, father decided that she deserved a new washing machine. For some reason this required a trip to Toronto which, although only thirty miles away, was a major expedition. That was the way Dad did things. We had gone with Dad's old gas-mask bag, allegedly a relic of his war experience, packed with sandwiches. It was the first time that I could recall being in a department store. We ascended by escalator up into the cavernous bowels of Eaton's. Dad warned me to 'step lively' at the top of each lift and terrified me by warning that my feet could be cut off if they became caught in the mechanism. I still possess a mild paranoia about escalators.

There was a vast and bewildering array of appliances. After what seemed like an interminable presentation by a clerk, my father settled on a Viking Brand wringer-washer. It would serve for the next thirty years and was always a vicious thing. One of my future chores was doing the laundry and I caught my hands several times in the rollers of the machine while wringing out clothing between tubs of rinse water. I can still see the Viking ship logo on the top of machine as it insidiously ingested my hand and arm while I desperately struggled to reach the lever that released the mechanism. I had nightmares about being dismembered in that contraption.

After the department store we went off to see the railway yards. My father loved trains and often stood for hours excitedly reviewing switches, engines, cars, and cabooses. He was an original train spotter and never understood why everyone else did not share his absolute ecstasy about seeing yet another damned train. On this occasion we stood on a bridge overlooking the yard, where we met a man who claimed to be a railway locomotive engineer. He seemed a god-like creature to me. A few steam locomotives were still in use at that time. They were huge, terrifying monsters to me and anyone who could control such a thing must possess special powers, in the same category as airplane pilots and mariners.

As the day wore on my father took me to the Royal Ontario Museum, a dark echoing place filled with wonders and terrors of every description. It is a fond memory of my father trying to do what he felt was right. He could not see, however, that I was overwhelmed and frightened, There were towering dinosaur skeletons, Egyptian mummies, stuffed dead animals everywhere, totem poles, halls filled with ancient weapons, clothing and miscellaneous artefacts. The place was enormous and my father dragged me through most of it in a few hours.

A startling memory of that visit was a bizarre assertion made by my father after we left the museum. As we sat resting at the end of a hall, eating our soggy Spam sandwiches from the gas-mask bag, my father told me that a woman had come and sat opposite him, then slowly raised her dress to reveal she was 'wearing nothing underneath'. Through the years my father would make many incongruous and inappropriate claims, often of a sexual nature. They would come at inopportune moments from no apparent motivation. I was always alert for the next potential embarrassment. I blanch yet as I consider that, even if this claim were true, it was not something that a rational man would mention to his four year old son.

Our day was not over yet. My father was unable to comprehend the limited endurance of a child and dragged me on to see or do something else when all I needed was a rest. This day yet included a trip to Center and Ward Islands in the Toronto harbour. It meant taking a wonderful ride on a wheezing ferry called the Sam McBride. Although I was exhausted, I loved that boat. It was exotic and mysterious, with polished wood, the gentle clanking of engine room telegraphs and the steadfast hissing of its steam engine. For some reason a huge halberd protruded from either end of the ferry, in front of each of its wheelhouses. The islands were idyllic, with plenty of water fowl, yet another of my father's fascinations. I remember white swans swimming through still waters under weeping willow trees and ducks everywhere. Another attraction of these islands was an airport. We sat and watched students of the Toronto Flying Club practise landings, bouncing yellow Piper Cubs high into the air above the runway. Despite the many bitter memories of my childhood there are also happy ones. Like a rare diamond, this day in Toronto was one.

Our little family went to the Canadian National Exhibition a few times, and there were several annual trips to the Royal Winter Fair, held on the same site. My parents fitted me with a harness on the end of a leash clipped to my father's belt. It was miserable tagging along like a dog, dragged at my father's pace through the jostling crowd, no matter how tired my small legs became. Nevertheless, the exhibition was a riot of colour, noise, activities and wide-eyed wonders. I remember a cut-away working model of an underground mine. Elevators rose and descended, underground machinery and railways were in constant motion, and tiny electric lights glowed everywhere in the mineshafts. Above ground, a model of life on the surface hummed busily above the troglodyte world beneath. It was an amazing feat of miniature mechanics and synchronization. I hope that somewhere, someone has preserved it.

Outside in the hot summer light a group of walnut-faced Huron Indians sat building genuine birch-bark canoes. Black kettles steamed over open campfires where the builders softened, bent and split the various natural woods used in their art. It was fascinating to recognize the beautiful form of a canoe emerging from a pile of sticks, roots and bark, without the benefit of any machinery. By contrast to this dying art, the growing affluence of the mid 1950's and ensuing fascination with gadgetry of all sorts offered something to fascinate everyone. There were halls filled with home appliances. I remember how we stood spellbound before a working display of automatic dishwashers, watching water swirl about and wondering, 'Whatever will they think of next?'

We once attended a live stage show at the exhibition. Secular events were entirely out of character for my parents. This was a life time event, hosted by Arthur Godfrey, a popular actor and personality of the time who, I was interested to learn, flew his own DC3 as he travelled around the continent. The only other interesting thing about that show was a film on a huge screen about the recent landfall of Marilyn   Bell as she completed her epic swim across Lake Ontario from Rochester to Toronto. That feat was accomplished a few weeks earlier in August 1954. She was sixteen years old.

The exhibition also had barns filled with every kind of farm animal. There were entire halls dedicated to poultry, as well as halls for sheep, for horses, for cattle, and for pigs. It was overwhelming and we saw it all. A few months later, the livestock shows would be repeated again at the Royal

Winter Fair. More farm animal displays and competitions combined with every conceivable contest possible. Best grain, best gourds, potatoes, carrots; every sort of fruit and vegetable was on show to be judged. Baking, quilting, tobacco, fleece and knitting, anything associated with agricultural life was on display. There were ploughing matches, milking competitions, sheep-shearing contests, equestrian events and endless other farmer fun activities. It was the ultimate country fall fair, presented on a provincial scale.

Occasionally we went to Riverdale Zoo in Toronto. Typically for our family it was a near Tolkeinian expedition. Nothing was ever a simple family outing. A day's preparation before, early to bed, early up and then a grinding bus ride into the city. The convoluted journey continued on subways and streetcars until we were finally at the zoo gates. We spent the day hiking around all the cages and enclosures, my father trying to make appropriate animal sounds for each species of creature, annoying and embarrassing everyone in his wake. At least one heated argument would arise between my parents, unable to go anywhere in public without a fight. I vaguely recall one spat had something to do with a masturbating monkey. By the end of the day I was exhausted, but there was still the return journey home to endure.

Once we took the family Studebaker into Toronto, but Dad had made a left turn through a red light and we had been grazed by a carload of excited, angry Italian men. They scared the hell out of him. After that, we travelled into the city only on public transit. Dad was not a brilliant driver despite his incessant ranting about other motorists. Mother was the quintessential back seat driver who nagged and worried incessantly; in moments of panic she would seize the steering wheel or other controls.

Across the street from our apartment, next to the fire hall, a post office was built while we lived there. I watched through the winter months as the foundations were dug and poured. Men slogged through the cold mud, pushing wheelbarrows and packing timber on their backs. Dad was one of them. It was the first permanent job he held, working on the project until it was finished. Then he found a position with the postal service as a mailman and he never quit. As strange a personality as he was, somehow he managed to persevere successfully among all the people he met daily. The only career counselling he ever offered was to get a job with the post office. The uniform, limited but steady pay, and prospects of a pension were a luxury compared to life as a farm labourer.

Some days my father took me into the Post Office, where the mail was sorted for delivery or shipping. It seemed a massive place to a young boy and there was a strange sense of order to the eternal bustle within the walls of this wholly government operated endeavour. At the time, dad held a sense of pride about 'neither rain, nor sleet, nor snow....' The huge building always had a strange smell, rather like the halls of the schools I attended but headier, more exotic. There was a sense of things from far-off places and of people's secret, personal business entrusted. It was after all, only the smell of mail and paper and ink and dust; but it was also the aroma of the real world and its commerce. My father took heady pride in his uniform and gleaned every possible nuance of power he perceived it gave him. He delighted in telling how he would, 'cut a street off.' This meant that he would not deliver mail to anyone on a street where he had encountered a threatening dog, or where the snow was not satisfactorily cleared from the front of a building. Despite his attitude he seemed to make many friends among the people to whom he delivered mail. At Christmas time he would be showered with gifts and cash. He also found extra income doing odd gardening jobs for some of these people although he often made enemies through his odd and often inappropriate bursts of bizarre behaviour.

.

A zealous lover of military music, dad once cajoled me into accompanying him to Maple Leaf Gardens in Toronto. Regimental military bands from Britain would march and play to the strange delight of an audience which thronged to see them. There had been an interlude with a car from a James Bond movie. It tore around inside the stadium spewing smoke, hidden machine guns blazing, and with a dummy that flew from its ejector seat. For a boy forbidden to see movies, it was no small thrill. Yes, there are pleasant memories. Thinly dispersed between the grim drudgeries of my daily existence they are unforgettable.

The last place where I lived with my father was in a tiny house on a small parcel of land that he rented for thirty-five years. I shudder to think of the investments and accrued interest that amount of rent money could have bought. I also know now that it is not unusual, especially for someone from Europe, to never own their home. Dad was a zealous gardener and had grand dreams of what he could do to the place. These dreams were fuelled by the arrangement he thought he had with the landlord. He had convinced himself that he would inherit the property when the ancient, heirless landlord died. Problem was - the old scrooge almost out-lived my father.

The lot was enclosed on two sides by the backyards of post-war-built homes, on another side by a retirement complex and on the fourth side sprawled a large public elementary school. I attended that school for several years and its immediate proximity to my house was a constant source of embarrassment and humiliation. Now I drove into the school yard and along the fence separating it from my old home. There was an open view of the yard from the entire south side of the school and I could see that little had changed, having last laid eyes on the place over a quarter of a century earlier. Although divorced from him, my father's second wife and a daughter by that marriage still lived on the property. Obviously its upkeep was beyond their abilities. About a half-acre in size, the lot was four times as long as it was wide. The garishly painted old house sat on the far end of a long lane that ran the full length of the property from the house out to the street after turning along the school fence.

I remembered the daunting task of shovelling snow. Sometimes two feet or more of wet, heavy slush from one storm had to be laboriously scraped and heaved onto the lawn the entire length of the drive, taking care not to scrape up any gravel from its surface, a mistake punishable with the usual ranting and beatings. When my family first moved there, we had migrated from the basement suite of a tenement building several blocks away. There were endless trips between the two places, transferring loads of belongings in my tired old wagon, the clack-clack of its wheels counting out the cracks in the sidewalks.

The new yard was covered in thick red clay, the same material that supplied several brick factories throughout the county. The muddy ruts to the house soon had Dad planning how to solve the problem. Others would have simply arranged for a truck to place gravel along the driveway, but not my father. With characteristic mad ambition he announced that, 'in England the Romans built roads that are still used two thousand years later.' He did not consider that those roads were main thoroughfares and had been built with slave labour. He had a perpetual need to build monuments; after living in an apartment he was bursting with bold dreams.

At that time the family vehicle was a badly rusted 1950's vintage Studebaker car, painted an ugly aqua colour. The worst rust-holes had been chiselled out and Dad had filled them in with pieces of galvanized roofing. The engine burned oil furiously and always trailed a thick cloud of bilious smoke. My father began excavating the driveway by hand to a depth of almost two feet. What he did with the excavations

I cannot recall, but I do remember that the Studebaker's trunk was used to haul home slabs of shale as big as my father could lift. They were fitted together in layers the entire length of the driveway, three or four hundred feet. Any regular madman would have contented himself with a single layer, but this project involved stacking several strata until the entire driveway was almost two feet deep with carefully fitted rocks. A finishing layer of fine gravel on top and the project had all the fragility of an airport runway. It had taken the damned fool almost a year of steady work. I mused that when the time comes to excavate the place for new development, there will be some very surprised people. I chuckled to think of archaeologists being summoned to decipher the meaning of this remarkable buried find.

On one side of the yard sat the stout and ugly garden shed, something I had helped build. I remember salvaging lumber from a derelict chicken coop and hauling it home. We pried the brittle slivered boards loose and scraped off layers of acrid manure. One of my tasks was salvaging and straightening the nails. My father had been determined that if we should move again he would not leave his garden shed behind, as we had always done in the past, so he ingeniously built it out of six panels that bolted together. Thirty-five years later it was still standing, looking solid and unmovable. Next to it sat an old van up on blocks, wheels removed and painted the same drab colour as the shed. Intended perhaps for use as a greenhouse, this van was typical of my father's penchant for the ugly and incongruous. Bemused, I considered that I needed a garden shed at my new house in British Columbia. Smiling to myself, I fleetingly considered the ludicrous plan of disassembling the shed and shipping it home, an ultimate souvenir for the son of the son.

Turning my attention to the school, I remembered sitting in these same classrooms. The antics at home unfolded beyond the windows and before the entire class. My mother was determined to learn to drive despite my father's strong admonishment that she did not have the basic, necessary intuitions. He was right. However, she was resolute and decided to teach herself some of the basics if no one else would. Somehow she procured a key for the car. On days when my father was at work, she began teaching herself, 'letting out the clutch, steering and backing up.' It took a lot of practice. By then there were huge vegetable gardens along the entire length of the driveway and a monstrous, drive-in compost bin at the end of the lot where the lane took a sharp turn along the school fence. Light poles had been installed at regular intervals along the driveway, so that my father could work in the garden at night. From my school desk I repeatedly watched in dread as mother began her ritual by warming up the car. Blue exhaust billowed upward. To my horror and the hysterical amusement of class and teacher, she soon had the old car lurching back and forth along the driveway, leaping and bucking frantically in clouds of smoke, careening wildly to stay on the track. Probably the suspension and the steering of the old wreck were completely worn out from its employment as dad's dump truck. With a badly sagging driver's seat, manual steering and my short mother peering through the large steering wheel, it was an unforgettable sight. One day a backing manoeuvre went wrong and the car ended up in the garden with furiously spinning rear wheels suspended over a lamppost that now tilted crazily. That night I returned home deliberately late; I cannot describe what sort of row there was between my parents. There must have been one. It would be several years before she finally acquired the coveted driving license and her wake of destruction would continue. That is another sad and uproariously funny story.

Meanwhile she rode diligently as co -pilot for my father, screeching hysterically, slamming her foot down on an imaginary brake pedal and randomly grabbing for the steering wheel. Dad was not a great driver, especially in city traffic and with the erratic distractions of mother trying to command the helm. It is a miracle that we survived any of our outings together in our family jalopies. Seatbelts and air-bags were then unknown.

Mother's Studebaker performance was an ultimate class-stopper but there was often something else going on at home that could be equally humiliating. My father had suspended speakers from his lamp posts. The lamps permitted him to work in the garden long after dark. He had eclectic tastes in sound entertainment, with a special delight in bird recordings, train recordings and military bands. He would put a stack of records on his 'hi-fi', and go to work in the potato patch. Occasionally he would procure a copy of sound effects and work blissfully under the blaring concert of an air battle or the screech of bag pipes or perhaps the squawking of some exotic goose. Peculiar sounds would emanate from the yard at impossible times of night or day. He must have been a great neighbour! Sitting in class, I'd squirm down in my seat when I saw my father appear in his garden on a day off. One day to my horror he began marching along the driveway, garden fork shouldered like a rifle, practising parade-square drill steps obviously inspired by whatever military band recording he had selected to play. Slack-jawed, the entire class and teacher sat in silence and watched the lengthy performance.

For obvious reasons I had a hard time integrating with other children. I had been an only child living in rural settings with no other children for miles around. My parents had few friends with whom they could interact. When we moved to town, I had few of the social skills necessary to interact with my peers. I was intelligent enough, and in a peculiar way had acquired some of the ignorant, fundamentalist arrogance from my parents that most people 'of the world' were fools and infidels. That did not prevent me from being the subject of constant bullying and taunting at school; I soon had to learn the rudiments of defending myself with my fists. My clothing was often odd, homemade and completely weird against the standards of my juvenile colleagues. I was provided with cheap, catalogue-ordered shoes purchased a few sizes too large so that I could 'grow into them'.

I would clomp off to school feeling that I was dressed like a clown and subjected to the enduring sarcasm of my classmates. As a youngster I did not enjoy good health, often suffering from long colds and so, from the first turning of leaves in autumn until the heat of early summer, my parents expected me to wear winter gear. Heavy boots, parkas, mitts and ugly fuzzy hats: none of these were worn by other kids except when actually demanded by the weather. I had a ritual of removing much of the cumbersome clothing as soon as I was out of sight of home, stuffing mitts into pockets, my bulky hat stowed inside a sleeve, trying my best to appear normal. At a loss about how to interact, I felt completely alienated from fellow students. Although I found ways of avoiding everyone until it was time to go into class, I always agonized in my role as a loner. Often the only friendships I developed were with a few other children who, for whatever reason, were also little odd sods who did not fit in.

For several years I wore the same old grey parka. As I grew, my mother kept extending the sleeves and hem with oddly matched bits of material. She was quite proud of her thrifty efforts. I would have been as embarrassed to go to school naked as I was to be seen wearing worn-out rags. In retrospect, the clothing did not matter. In fact, a few years later that sort of attire would have been considered cool. What was unforgivable was my parents' deliberate disregard and blatant ignorance about the social pressures I endured because of them. They would at times insist that it was virtuous to be apart from the children of 'the world', a fundamentalist term that implied that the status quo was inherently evil.

The time spent on my own allowed me to become very observant. If I could not participate, I could watch and absorb. Decades later my powers of observation have developed with the curse of an indelible memory and a stupendous array of unwanted details. I often wonder if, in the fog of time, my memories are skewed and inaccurate. However, each detail I saw conjured up yet another indelible crystalline image from the past.

The principal of this school had been a man named Mr. Balfour, a lanky man with wavy hair and goggle-like eyeglasses. Educators were pillars of the community, whom I had been taught to fear and respect. The other prominent figure at that school was the caretaker, Mr. Boyd. He was a big man, older, slow-moving, yet it seemed he did all the cleaning, repair and maintenance work single-handedly throughout the entire school. He used to mow the vast lawns of the school on an ancient and fascinating riding lawnmower that sported a huge brass turtle's head over the name 'Snapper'. He keep the furnace running, the halls and washrooms spotlessly clean, and the windows washed. He raised and lowered the flag daily and always had time for a friendly greeting despite his eternal agenda.

Mr. Boyd kept two flags fluttering from the school flag-pole, a Union Jack and an Elmer-the-Safety-Elephant flag. The later was a green triangular cloth with a little elephant that wore a silly pointed hat. If the flag flew, it meant that everyone had been following Elmer's traffic safety rules and no-one had been injured while walking to or from school. This was street-proofing of the day. The safety program was administrated by a huge policeman named Constable Hook, who provided seminars for fledgling schoolchildren with tiny traffic lights, cars that the children could pedal and Elmer traffic safety colouring books. The class would joyously chant, 'Good morning Constable Hook', and then sit in wide-eyed wonder learning about all the ways we could be decimated in traffic.

While in kindergarten at another school, I crossed a busy street twice daily and had one day leapt out between parked cars, a cardinal Elmer felony. I found myself in the path of a huge green Chevy bearing down on me with the screech of skidding tires and the horror-stricken faces of two elderly women in the windshield. The car had come to a stop with my upraised hands resting lightly on either side of the hood ornament. I was unscathed but can still see those faces. Two classmates who had seen the incident threatened to tell the teacher, so that the Elmer flag would have to be lowered. I was more mortified about this possible consequence than I was about my close brush with death.

Presently I was recalling events from my first year in school. I attended kindergarten under the tutelage of an albino woman named Miss May. The building was very old and the walls filled with rats. Often the class could hear them scuttling and gnawing throughout the building. Miss May wore dark glasses to hide her colourless eyes. Every day the children were required to roll out a towel and have a brief nap. One little urchin managed to pee herself nearly every nap time. One day, in a fury Miss May removed her glasses to glare at the little girl. It was a miracle that at the sight of her strange rabbit pink eyes, my entire class of tots did not piss themselves. It was a wonderful time for me, feeling 'grown-up' because I now went to school. The lofty, echoing grandeur of the old building, the comforting weight of books, the smell and taste of mucilage, those few all-too-brief hours each day when I was out of my parents' grasp, surrounded by rational adults who seemed to care about me, were a magic that would elude me by the time I attended that school next door to my house.

By first grade, I had already begun to find myself alienated and felt at times like a freak. It was frustrating beyond words to feel utterly alone among my peers. Acceptance is such a vital thing to a child. My parents did not or could not understand. It was clear to me that they were indeed 'freaks'. It followed in my mind that I was their progeny. I have never been able to outgrow the sense that I am not adequate and somehow do not deserve a status quite as high as my fellows. I know that is ludicrous, but it is nearly impossible to perform outside that membrane of self-deprecation which exists undeniably in the deepest recesses of my being. It was placed there inexorably and methodically (although I believe innocently), during the entire formative period of my youth. Then my parents left me to my own devices. Nearly every achievement in my life has been made with a conscious effort to overcome an extremely negative instinct. What I can apply to my intellect, I cannot modify in my soul.

For some reason I got along quite well with many of the girls during those early school years and, while I was often ostracized by the boys because of my association with girls, risking the dreaded fictitious disease called 'cooties', I quite enjoyed a singular and exclusive familiarity with some of the female student body. This included pre-pubescent 'doctor games', show and giggle encounters that were pleasantly naughty. Terrified of being found out, I also felt quite smug, aware that my budding sexual accomplishments, such as they were, far outweighed those of any of the boys. Somehow the secret remained intact.

I began reading voraciously. Half-way through the first grade I had devoured all of the Dick and Jane texts, Cat in the Hat, and Curious George books available. Upon learning about the local library and the concept of borrowing books, I persuaded my mother to let me visit regularly. I once arrived in a grade one class to give a book report as requested by the teacher. The book I had lugged to school was the 'Iliad of Homer', I could read little of it and understood even less, but the teacher was so impressed that the following year I was 'accelerated' and took grades two and three studies in the same year. Taunted by the older kids in my class, I persevered successfully with my academics but continued to fail miserably outside the classroom.

As an adult and a parent, now married to a school teacher, I am convinced that children in a school environment must learn how to interact others, both with their peers and authority figures. Dignity is far more important than any academic pursuit. With good self-esteem and a desire to learn, a true education will necessarily follow. Having acquired a thirst for knowledge, I wish that human interaction was what I'd learned first. Maybe I just did not have a chance with what I faced at home.

I was often called a 'browner', a term which accused me of 'brown-nosing', synonymous with 'ass licking', or trying too hard to please my teachers. I had been permanently labelled with my nickname 'farmer', a huge insult at that time, and I often endured gang-like beatings from some of the bigger boys. I would go home, battered and bloodied, sometimes with torn clothes, some items of apparel even stolen by other kids. Then I would have to endure screaming interrogations from my parents which often ended with another beating.

In spring time, the schoolchildren tried breaking the ice on top of the ditches. It could be dangerous; if the ditch was deep, a youngster could fall through the ice and be drawn underneath by the swiftly running drainage. The most common mishap was when someone ended up with a 'soaker', which was when you filled your boots with water. Of course this activity was strictly forbidden by everyone's parents, especially mine. Nevertheless occasionally overcome by temptation, I eventually returned home with the inevitable wet foot and suffered the consequences.

A memorable beating came on a day when I had neither been playing on the ditches nor had come home via the route as accused by my father. Denying that I had come home on that particular street was justification for an especially vigorous beating. This was usually a whipping with a leather belt on my bare backside, often until blood was drawn. I never knew whether to cry out or remain silent. Depending on the mood of my father, one reaction or the other would draw yet more strokes of the belt as well as punches and kicks. 'I'll give you something to scream about', or "'Think you're a tough little bugger, we'll see how you like this!' were routine reactions that accompanied the thrashings. On several occasions my father would hold his massive fists to my face and tell me how he had been trained to 'kill people with these bare hands, so don't get smart with me!' There was one occasion when I was beaten until severely bloodied, then had a bottle of rubbing alcohol poured on my raw buttocks just to show me how the fires of hell would feel if I didn't mend my ways. Finally I was physically thrown out into the backyard with only a burlap sack to cover myself, and tied to an apple tree for the night. This was done so that as a six-year-old I would know what it was like to be a 'hobo', which was what would soon happen to me if I did not stop being so 'cantankerous'. As usual I wasn't sure what I had done to provoke any punishment, especially something so callously sadistic.

I cared little about pleasing either parent but went about my duties at home contritely and joylessly. All I ever wanted to do was to avoid the next beating. Often, whatever was now wrong proved to be exactly the opposite of what I had been previously punished for. Both parents participated in my ordeals and, as far as I could recall, they both used their classic lines about 'spare the rod and spoil the child', and

'This is hurting me a lot more that you'.   Right!   The psychological beatings were incessant and horrific.   No amount of adult rationalization can alleviate a permanently induced sadness.

During those long, tortured childhood years, my parents also fought constantly, often violently. Through the various rented homes we occupied (we were often asked to move after an especially violent bout), came an endless procession of clergymen, doctors, police and social workers. There were terrifying fights in the middle of the night, broken dishes and furniture, spattered blood. The shattering crashes, dull thud of landed blows, shouted threats and screams will always echo in my memory. If all the violence failed to win the persuasions intended by either of my parents, they would each on occasion resort to threats of suicide. 'If you don't stop making my life so miserable, I may as well kill myself!' Those threats were often directed at me. As a boy I was at times left feeling responsible for their continued existence. There were times when I was disappointed that they did not put themselves out of their misery and out of mine.

Another declaration my parents each used was to tell me that, 'You're just like your bloody father' or 'mother', as the case might be.   When their frustration with each other overwhelmed them, blame was thrust upon me, and eventually my sister.   My programming began early and effectively.   To this day, in any imperfect situation, I will assume guilt regardless of whoever is actually at fault, or even if no-one need be blamed.   At times it is an easy way to resolve an issue, but permanent guilt for all the woes in the world is a tiresome load.

Eventually   the   notion   of   suicide   became   a programmed reaction to any crisis. I have gone through my entire life instinctively considering self-destruction whenever any situation appears to be hopeless or too difficult to bear. I never actually tried to end my life, swallowed the pills, pulled the trigger, flicked my wrist while driving past an abutment, but I cannot shake off the haunting, dark notions. It is part of the curse that is my legacy. Most tragically when I find myself floundering in my deepest, darkest despair is the time when I also lose control to the point of threatening suicide to those who do indeed love me. (At moments like that, their affection is beyond my comprehension.) It is a horrible anguish to hear myself uttering completely irrational threats. The pain I have caused those souls whom I most needed is incalculable. There are so many I eventually drove away, perhaps now harbouring their own dark despair and guilt. At times, it has only been their love that has sustained me. When I think of how I have treated them, the shame of it can drive me into yet another dark despair; and more guilt. It is a black hole of frustration and darkness. Escape seems impossible. How did the chain become forged so cleverly, so fucking unbreakably? Whose father first imposed this horror on his son, unknowing or uncaring about the inheritance of the sins of his fathers and how like a stone tossed into a large pond, its ripples expand eternally outward, corrupting the entire family tree. Like a deadly virus, eventually everyone is infected and their lives permanently affected.

Bitterly I recalled that despite all the temporary homes to which I had been whisked away during yet another crisis, I was always returned to the same environment. How my sister and I survived in any sense was a sad miracle. I learned in later years that an aunt had desperately tried to adopt both of us in order to remove us from our entrapment. Yet, when my mother finally left my father and the family officially broke apart, she claimed to have pleaded vigorously with a local judge to prevent her children from become wards of what was then called 'Children's Aid'. When I later learned that my sister and I were so close to being salvaged from our misery, I would bitterly castigate my mother for her selfishness. But then, perhaps we could have ended up in an environment that was even worse. I remain bitter about all of those in a position to help who, knowing our plight, did nothing to remove my sister and me. That still occurs today, with tragic results both immediately and often for the rest of a miserable life.

As an adult I slowly realized that I have a dysfunctional personality and would continue to have extreme difficulty dealing with life and other people if I did not make changes. I feared that I was becoming just like my parents. Finally admitting to myself that I was powerless to effect change on my own, I conceded the need for professional help, especially when the family doctor suggested that regular thoughts of suicide were not normal for the average, healthy person. I was diagnosed as being manic depressive, in all probability an inherited genetic disorder that is imminently treatable. With medication I was able to begin sorting out my learned behaviours from those that were simply my natural personality. Acknowledging a need for help was the largest most difficult step in finding a resolution. Once I accepted the notion that my problem should be no more stigmatic than any medical disorder, I was, for the first time in my life, able to feel that I could look the world in the eye and smile back. That felt good!

I shook myself from my dark thoughts and began to walk around the school grounds, trying to remember something pleasant. This was the schoolyard where I had played and fought with the other kids, or lurked alone in a remote corner. For years I had a recurring dream about running across this very field, slowly and effortlessly rising into the air to glide in serene amazement, detached from the heaviness of life. I walked slowly, amazed at the sharpness of the memories, recalling names of classmates and incidents from so long ago. This was the corner where I'd had a snowball fight with Benny Devitto. I was hit in the eye with a snowball packed around a chunk of ice; several stitches were needed to close the gaping wound. 'Where are you now?' I thought, 'you little bastard!' Thirty-five years later I was wondering what had become of Benny and my other classmates, amazed at how readily some of their names came back to me.

I wandered slowly past the classroom windows. This room was where I had spent an eternity in a single sleepy spring afternoon, the warm sun beaming through the window, smells of mud and new grass perfuming the air, watching robins pull worms from the soft ground, the teacher's voice a soft, sleepy drone far away. Here was the woodworking shop where I had built a crude crystal radio set and there was Miss Douglas' room, a torture chamber of multiplication, square roots and geometry.

Air raid drills were a regular routine. I attended classes here during the height of the Cold War and the terror of the Cuban Missile Crisis. Sirens would begin to howl at random times, and we all ducked under our desks as we had been trained and waited for the all-clear signal or a devastating explosion. As the threat of a missile attack was ever present, many people had resolved themselves to the inevitability of annihilation. Nuclear holocaust was an accepted fact of life, ads for survival kits and bomb shelters were common everywhere. For me, it was just another dark cloud in my existence. I had been hearing about Armageddon my whole life. On a sunny Autumn afternoon, a few years later in this same school, Friday November 22, 1963, Mr. Balfour interrupted classes with the intercom announcement that John F. Kennedy had been shot. Days later, the entire school would gather in the auditorium to watch the funeral procession on a huge black and white television. Many were in tears, despite the mystery of the event's significance to us youngsters.

I drove out of the school grounds, weary with my

memories and the burden of the daunting chores that lay ahead, but I still had time to kill. I was waiting to meet with the caretaker of my father's apartment. I travelled around the neighbourhood, retracing the route where I so often walked aimlessly and incessantly, alone in the dark, passing the time until I could go home tired enough to sleep. After mother had taken my sister and moved out, I seemed to be of only nuisance value to my father. I would wander the streets aimlessly, passing as much time away from the house as possible.

I had once delivered newspapers, an idea inspired by my mother. She declared that it would be an excellent way for me to learn responsibility and to acquire financial management skills. What I learned indelibly was to spend any money I had before someone else got their hands on it. I had taken on the daily delivery of the Toronto Telegram on a winding route that swelled to one hundred and twenty customers on Saturdays. The weekend papers weighed several pounds each, which meant that I had almost a quarter ton of newsprint to circulate, no matter what the weather was like, how late the delivery truck was, or what else I would rather be doing. Often the papers were too heavy to deliver all at once. I transported them on my old bike, towing the faithful wagon. My parents never helped. I had to leave some of the papers on the curb, returning to pick them up after the first part of the route was delivered. Sometimes the papers had vanished by the time I returned, or they would be muddy or wet from rain and snow. Then I would have to go to the door of each of my customers trying to explain why they did not have their evening paper, no easy chore for a boy as introverted as I was!

Twice a month, Saturday mornings were devoted to collecting money from my customers, scheming ways to catch up with those who were never home. Then I had to go home and count out the money and prepare a bank deposit for the newspaper agent. My mother insisted on involving herself in the process, extracting a percentage for her services and another for the collection plate at church. This I would be sure to pocket later. I was forced to go to church in silly, ill-fitting clothes several times a week. I would be damned if I was giving away any of my hard-won earnings to an institution I despised. It was a small way of feeling that I had some control over my life. Since I could not purchase anything obvious with the funds that I purloined from myself, I spent them frivolously but retained the dignity of quiet spite. It never occurred to me to save my funds in a safe place.

Spending money recklessly would become a lifelong curse. I have never acquired money management skills and am eternally broke, despite at times earning fantastic incomes. The one time in my adult life that I had developed financial security, it was all whisked away as a result of a bad marriage. This experience only confirmed my instinct to spend my money as quickly as possible.

As I approached middle age I finally began to realize how desperate my finances were and that they would become worse in old age if I did not change my methods. My father had hopelessly floundered from one debt to another despite the assistance of friends and relatives. It is a symptom of manic depression, uncontrolled spending that somehow gives the sufferer a temporary sense of well-being. 'So long as I am able to acquire, I am OK'. Ultimately the amassed debts incur a bottomless depression that induces more manic activity, which in one way or another leads to even further debt. This curse I know is not unique to me, yet I struggle to break the pattern and find the freedom which I so desperately crave. It is a terrible to realize that you are a prisoner of yourself. We all are to some degree. In today's consumer society with its strip mall mentality, perhaps we have all been manipulated into permanent depression as we strive to look like that, smell like this, drive one of those and have whatever, or whomever, we want on a whim.

Whatever time was left after my paper route was devoted to household chores: cooking for my mother, and yard and garden labour for dad. I was expected to fulfill my duties at home as a priority over anything else in my life, even school. If I protested there would be added labour to accompany the expected beating. 'Idle hands find the devil's work' was something my mother would tell me when I complained, which did not explain why her children did most of her work for her. Fortunately, I found school work easy and, with whatever time I had left to myself, I would soon be as far away from home as possible. Boredom was never a problem for me; all the things I wanted to do provided incentive to accomplish the work at hand as soon as possible. I also managed to salvage time for myself in the gaps provided by the ongoing domestic battles. My parents clung to routines. Monday was always laundry day, Friday was grocery shopping day, and Saturday was for house cleaning yard work. There was even a weekly routine about meals, the basic family menu revolving around seven recipes: Monday was macaroni and hamburgers, and so on through Sunday, each day having its specific menu. . For a long time, the family subsisted on watery soups made from cabbage and turnips while most of the grocery money went to television evangelists.

That first day in Oakville wore on like eternity itself. In one afternoon I had reviewed a large portion of my first sixteen years and was exhausted from the effort. Yet time seemed to stand still. An hour remained before I could meet my father's landlord and obtain the keys to the apartment. I drove on a few blocks to another area we had lived when I was just beginning my school years.

I had no trouble finding the lot where our old rented shack had once stood, but a new house now occupied the same space. I remembered a huge vegetable garden in the back. Across the street a large park separated us from the back of the civic arena where a circus came annually. Each year my father would wheelbarrow many steaming loads of manure across the park to his garden, jovially extolling the value of elephant shit. Smiling to myself, I vaguely recalled a photograph of me standing beneath the broad leaves of some monstrous plant, solid proof of the potent properties of exotic dung. At the back of the garden my father built a fence that seemed ten feet high, as well as yet another garden shed to block out the curious observations of neighbours as he went about his strange industries.

One of the churches we attended had acquired some land and was about to begin building a new facility. My father undertook the removal of an old chicken coop that stood in the middle of the site and I helped him disassemble it under a blistering summer sun. Every splintery board was salvaged, scraped of its acrid coating of choking, dusty chicken manure. Every nail was pried loose, straightened and sorted. It was horrible, back-breaking work. Once the dismantling was completed, the material was hauled home and reassembled as a large shed. Father was a master of masochism, sadism and false economy. He was always able to find a way of squandering time, effort and money in an attempt to create an illusion of saving a few dollars.

Even though this was the same backyard where I been tied to the tree, I recalled a happy memory. By that same apple tree I once stood with my parents under a starry autumn night sky. On October 4, 1957 we stared into the clear night sky along with all the other people on the street. The Soviet satellite, Sputnik, had been launched a few hours earlier. We were all in our backyards peering up, not sure what we were looking for. The world had been advised by the media that Sputnik could be seen by the naked eye and would resemble a small star travelling rapidly across the firmament. Finally came a distant shout, then frantic visual straining, until one by one rose the exultant cry: 'I can see it!', whether they could or not. I did see it and knew even then that this was an event which changed history. The space age had begun. A timeless mystery now began to unravel as man began to find his way back to a distant calling from among the stars. My parents were more concerned about the ramifications of communist technology passing unrestricted over our heads. The only thing in their fundamentalist doctrine more evil than Catholicism was communism.

The family had moved here a few weeks after the birth of my sister, in the same month I had begun school. All these years later I marvelled at how far I had to walk to school alone, musing that today's parents accompany their children to kindergarten and grade school even if only across a street. I surmised that my parents had not been especially astute about child rearing and probably entrusted my care as much to God. Was it a different world then where people assumed that everyone looked out for children and few evils lurked to prey on the innocent? In retrospect, little has changed except society's awareness and perception. The danger had always existed. Nevertheless, most harm befell me once I was 'safely' at home.

I had a few friends on this street, children of a similar age. A brother and sister named Zigmus and Sigutas had a colour television in their family room. At that time, colour television was in its infancy, exotic expensive hi-technology. The colour was essentially monochromatic, but the tones could be changed from red to blue to green. All through suburbia people climbed onto rooftops to install new colour antennas. Cable signals were still unimagined future technology at a time when people took tubes from their television sets to the local hardware store for testing and replacement. Some TVs took several minutes to warm up enough for the picture to appear, and one became an expert at adjusting the picture with several knobs on both the front and back of the set. When televisions were turned off, the picture would slowly fade as the picture tube de-energized, and then it would shrink into a tiny, bright dot in the middle of the oval screen.

When I was not allowed into my friend's house, I would creep into their backyard and watch cartoons through a basement window. They would leave the television on for me while they ate supper. Further up the street I befriended another little girl, whose father was a bulk-petroleum dealer and had several barrels of various lubricants stored in his garage. One day while exploring there, I stepped on a loose lid that flipped up, tumbling me into a barrel filled with thick, dark, reeking gear oil. I hurried for home and for months later, my oily black footprints could still be seen in the cement of the sidewalk. The scolding about ruining a pair of my pants was severe: I was stripped and scrubbed with a stiff brush in a tub of hot water in the backyard.

We had lived here at the beginning of the cold war. There was escalating speculation about a nuclear attack. Everyone lived with this silent terror, including youngsters like myself. A massive information campaign previewed the dire effects of nuclear holocaust and outlined the few precautions that people could take. It produced a generation of paranoid people who in later years would develop into an insular society. We now accept fear and mistrust as a healthy attitude. In a strange way my fundamentalist parents were years ahead of their time in the manner that they embraced apocalyptic doctrines and were suspicious of the world in general.

This was also the era when natural gas was being installed throughout the town and there were problems. One morning a home with a new gas furnace, only a few blocks away, exploded without warning. Terrified, I thought that *the* bomb had just been dropped. I waited in screaming horror for the fiery wind that would flatten my home and burn me instantly to a crisp. Only hours later, after the sirens of emergency vehicles had long ceased their wailing, did I begin to suspect that life might go on. My parents found it hilarious that I had been so terrified. They teased me about that morning for months after: 'Look out, the bomb will get you!' These were the same people who delighted in trying to interpret the Book of Revelations and speculate about the horrors of Armageddon. What could possibly be amusing about a child's terror?

This little house held some fond memories too. A favourite uncle would visit us, usually for Christmas and sometimes in mid summer. He always brought gifts for me and exuded an air of worldliness that was exotic and intoxicating. He slept on the top mattress of the old army bunk bed in my room. I would lie awake listening to him snore, smelling the perfume of his sweat and tobacco. I was mesmerized by the notion that someone I idolized seemed to like me in return and, in fact, came back repeatedly to visit. One summer he showed up in a brand new Monarch convertible, a massive automobile even by late 1950's standards. The entire family went for a drive with the top down, stopping at a drive-in restaurant along the way. The magic of that day lingered until I was old enough to buy my own convertible and discover all the associated problems.

The bunk bed reminded me that I been quite sickly as a child, suffering from terrible colds and many childhood afflictions. Mother would drape the bunk bed with blankets and force me to stay in it for hours with a 'Vicks Vaporizer'. This was a large electric bottle that emitted a jet of steam over a tiny reservoir containing Vicks Vapour Rub. Whether or not it was an effective treatment was entirely speculative, but to the present day, I retch at the smell of Vicks and the taste of Buckley's Cough Mixture.

The park across the street was large enough to accommodate several sport events at once. A wooded ravine ran along one perimeter and it was a favourite place for children to play, affording a sense of being deep in the woods but within shouting distance of home. Along the opposite side of the park ran an entire, long, double row of yellow brick, three story apartment buildings. In the far corner of the park, between the last apartment block and the arena on the far side, was an outdoor swimming pool and recreation facility.

Little had changed. The field was full of people playing soccer. There were games in progress all over, filling the park with swarthy men shouting in Italian and Portuguese. Today, a sunny Sunday afternoon, was a timeless scene, as if it were perfectly rehearsed to confirm my memory. My parents regarded Sunday as a day of rest, literally. No matter what the season or weather, the ritual was the same. Upon returning from church, lunch was served, always a routine of bacon and eggs, then we had to retire for a long nap. I would sit at my bedroom window watching the soccer games across the street as the afternoon's eternal minutes slowly dragged by. Sunday supper was usually a snack of soda crackers, celery sticks with Cheese Whiz spread on them, followed by a bowl of Jell-O, usually made as thinly as possible: the ultimate pious repast. After the evening meal we all went back to church again.

For reasons I have forgotten, the family moved from our little house on the north side of the park into one of those apartments on the other side. It was a two bedroom basement suite. My sister and I shared the bunk bed in one small room; our window faced an alley where cars parked. In winter, the room would reek of exhaust fumes every morning as the tailpipe of an idling vehicle blasted the window. One morning my sister vanished. She always rose with dad and joined him at the breakfast table for a while. Not appearing as usual, she was checked upon but was not in her bed. Soon everyone was awake, combing the tiny apartment and frantically calling her. She was finally discovered standing behind the bathroom door, hiding under towels on a rack. There was no reason for the prank. She was just curious to see what everyone would do if they thought she was gone. Perhaps she wondered if she would be missed at all. As I stood surveying these dreadful tenements, I remembered the reek of burning garbage, and how sometimes, trash would catch fire in the chute that descended from each floor to the incinerator in the basement. I also remembered the echoing, stinking hallways, the dark, frightening communal storage area across the corridor in the basement and the human derelicts who often loitered in the foyer and entrance ways.

My mother's furious temper was not reserved exclusively for her own children. There was at least one occasion when she accosted and beat a child outside for doing something insignificant that had stirred her violent rage. There was a youngster named Alan, memorable because of his huge ears. He had been bouncing a ball against the wall of an adjacent building with his hockey stick when mother had taken it from him and began whacking him across his back because his 'racket' was annoying her. The boy's father was a co-worker of my father and the ramifications were huge. Yet somehow, she was never charged with assault. How times have changed! Today she would have been incarcerated for simply threatening a child. Everywhere we lived, something always occurred that precipitated yet anther move. My parents could not get along with anyone. The close quarters of apartment living were not a good place for these deliberate misfits and after two years we moved to the rental property where my father stayed for nearly the rest of his life.

Across the street from the apartment there stood a community swimming pool. My mother had decided that, since I was drawn to water, I should have swimming lessons. She enrolled me in a brief course one summer. The chlorinated pool water was always frigid and the instructors did more to terrify me of drowning than teach me about swimming. It took many years before I overcame the dread they instilled in me that summer and began to feel truly comfortable when 'out of my depth'.

In later years as a teenager at the same facility, I would attend weekly air cadet parades and rose to the lofty rank of warrant officer. It would prove to be a valuable facet of my life, offering structure, camaraderie and a flickering self-esteem. There was incessant marching, classes about firearms handling and most importantly, basic aviation instruction. Star cadets went on to earn their civilian pilot's license. There was also opportunity to spend summers on the Air force base near Trenton, learning leadership skills and spending time flying in military aircraft. I nearly enlisted in the regular armed forces, but was distracted by other opportunities.

Past the pool stood the arena where the Shriner's circus came each year. My mother was always concerned about the Circus Gypsies, convinced they looked for children to kidnap. Although I was free to wander the cages and trailers assembled behind the arena, my sister was guarded closely all the time that the troupe was there. I was fascinated with the animals and the circus people, secretly longing to be abducted and whisked away to strange places and new adventures. Carnivals also came to the park. For a few nights each year the whirling, brightly lit rides with their cacophony of sounds would take over the night. I would wander through the carnival, astonished at everything I saw, basking in the glittering worldliness. Oddly, what I now remember most vividly about those carnivals were the nighthawks. The carnivals had one or two huge searchlights that cast their intense, rotating beam up into the night sky. The lights would attract swarms of insects and several nighthawks would dive down the revolving beams feeding on the swarms, recovering from their dives with a loud zooming buzz.

I walked around the corner of the field, lost in my reveries, pausing briefly to stand beside the bleachers of the softball diamond. Nothing seemed to have changed. I smiled as I recalled salvaging cigar butts discarded under this same bleacher. I would take them and crawl beneath an overturned boat in the backyard next door to the apartment. I hid the butts there until I acquired a box of matches and then smoked myself into a nauseous haze. It was amusing to realize that I did because my parents would have vehemently disapproved.

Chapter Three

Gloom with a View

Finally the hour arrived to meet my father's landlord. I was exhausted, overwhelmed by the recollections that I had crowded into the front of my brain in the past few rushed hours. Now I had a rising urge to run, to abandon all this bittersweet experience and the drudgery that I knew was imminent. Why had I felt so obliged to come and do this thing? I owed my father nothing. Perhaps I was only here to assuage any possible future guilt if I ignored this last opportunity to display concern and a sense of family toward my father. I had had enough for one day, yet there was a burden of unknown responsibility waiting with the acquisition of one single key. Christ-weary, I shouldered my cross and rang the buzzer by the front door.

The apartment manager was a pleasant young man with a thick Russian accent. Greg and his wife had immigrated to Canada from the Soviet Union a few years previously and possessed the optimism and benevolence typical of many newly arrived from an oppressed society. Greg and my father had become friends through a mutual interest in railroading and my father's insistence at helping with the gardening around the apartment building. It was typical of Dad, who alienated himself from so many, to also be gregarious and helpful in the extreme with other people.

Greg reviewed the events of the past few months. It soon became clear that had it not been for his concern about the old man, my father would have died alone in his apartment. Elated that someone had finally come to take charge of the situation, Greg offered every possible assistance and when queried about overdue rent, he assured me that the damage deposit would cover what was unpaid if the apartment were cleaned and vacated by month's end. My father's vehicle was parked outside. Greg had been using it but offered me those keys along with the one for the apartment and two large boxes of accumulated mail.

I waited for the elevator to take me to the sixth floor. My trepidation rose and I still fought the urge to abandon the entire effort with the same indifference that I had so often endured from my father. The hallway reeked of stale cigarette smoke, something else that might have been urine and other insidious human malodours. The elevator smelled even worse. The building was obviously a low step above being a tenement and my sense of despair deepened. Finally I stood in front of the apartment door, poised with the key in my hand. Slowly I inserted it in the lock and, ignoring my misgivings, turned the handle and pushed the door open. I gasped and nearly staggered backward from the stench.

The place was a shambles and reeked horribly. Holding my breath, I rushed to the balcony door and flung it open. I did the same with the bedroom window and was appalled at what I found. The cloying stench had me suspecting that a body was somewhere in the apartment. What I found was nearly as bad. Leering at me from the window was a life-sized photo of my father he had taped to the glass for some inexplicable reason. Several other signs indicated a final madness had consumed the man. There were heaps of filthy clothing and bedding and, smeared everywhere, dried faeces. It was on the walls, in the bathtub, the sink and mirror, and caked on the tiled floor. It covered the living room walls, the entire dining room and smothered the floor and counter in the kitchen. Even dishes and utensils had a coating of my father's dried shit. Outside on the balcony, an inch-deep crust of pigeon droppings coated the deck and furniture. Gasping, fighting tears of horror and revulsion, I recalled how fastidious my father had always been. No matter what else he had not been, he was always scrupulously tidy. The one bedroom apartment looked as if it had contained a frustrated bear.

Obviously, as my father's condition declined, he had been reduced to crawling around the apartment, probably out of his mind, incontinent, blind, and incapable of feeding himself or even using the telephone to summon help. It was a hell of a way for anyone to end their life, no matter what they might deserve. 'Well old boy', I mused to myself: 'He was always giving you shit about something, you should be used to it. It's time to roll up your sleeves. At least this is one mess you *can* clean up!'

It took seven hours of scraping, scrubbing and disinfecting until finally the little apartment was fit for human habitation. Twenty-eight garbage bags were filled with dung-crusted, filthy bedding, clothing, spoiled food and miscellaneous corruption. There was a heap of mail that was irrelevant to any of my father's immediate affairs after a preliminary sorting. I went out again and spent a small fortune on cleaning supplies, garbage bags and new bedding. Finally the job was finished. Too late in the evening to find a restaurant still open, too tired to care, I returned to the apartment satisfied that it was now sanitary enough to sleep there without contracting a serious disease. I had thrown out the bed as it was too disgusting to use. I collapsed on the couch, so exhausted I could not sleep, and lay there long into the night, while wild thoughts raced through my weary head.

Slowly daylight came. Still unable to sleep, I rose and stepped out on the balcony, savouring the perfume of the early morning; it was comforting, an old familiar friend, the smell of home. I immediately realized why my father had rented this particular apartment. It commanded an excellent view of the property where he had lived and gardened for so long. Nothing could happen there which would escape his notice. I knew how much he must have missed his gardens, but I also knew that he would have constantly surveyed the activities of his estranged wife and their daughter. It was chilling to consider what it must be like to have someone who was potentially dangerous watching you all the time. It would be an eternal, ominous presence. What would have been especially frustrating was that there was no legal recourse. A man cannot be charged for renting a home.

I turned my attention to the affairs at hand, trying to prioritize the events of the day ahead. There was an apartment to vacate, junk to be sorted from valuable items and arrangements made to give away or ship significant articles to the right people. There was paper work to deal with, accounts to organize and close, a power of attorney document to be completed, funeral arrangements to be made for the imminent event. There were also relatives arriving from Britain. It was Monday morning. I had planned on flying home to British Columbia on Thursday but realized that I would have to delay the flight for a few days. Musing that elephants are eaten one bite at a time, I focused on my first priority, breakfast.

The day soon became a blur of frenetic activity. After a large meal I went to the hospital to visit my father and meet his doctor. Delighted that I had come back, dad thought that I had already returned home to the West coast. He was confused about virtually everything, and it took time and patience to deal with him. At times petulant and violent, he would rapidly lax into a subdued and passive state, often beginning to reminisce about something long ago and entirely forgotten. He was convinced that he was considerably older than his seventy-three years, and repeatedly claimed to be one hundred. He doggedly clung to the notion that the hospital staff could not be trusted, and that they deliberately kept the lights turned off so he could not see what they were doing or feeding him. Clearly, the old man teetered on the edge of lucidity, unable to separate reality from his fantasies. He lay there in his bed, a catheter running out of his penis into a bag hung on the side of the bed. It seemed ironic that the now shrivelled organ which had once inspired so much of his impetuous thinking was now no more than a piece of redundant plumbing.

My first order of business was necessarily completing the power of attorney documents. I could not do much to put affairs in order without that bit of paperwork. The problem was that my father was too blind to see and obviously not of sound mind and body but there was no choice but to fudge things along and hope for the best. Having acquired the necessary blank documents from the hospital administration office, I set about having my father practice signing his signature as best possible. I placed a pen in his hand and guided it across a page repeatedly. There was a question of witnesses. To my utter frustration, no-one employed by the hospital, or involved in his care, could legally witness my father's signature. I was at an impasse before I had begun.

Finally I realized that the hospital was full of other people who were visiting patients. Eventually I intercepted two who were sympathetic to my problem and willing to be witnesses. While the entire convoluted process unfolded, father sat in a wheelchair in the hospital corridor, with a blissful smirk on his face, starring blankly into oblivion, all the while practising various animal sounds. After enduring yet another round of 'quacks' and 'oinks', I looked up from these documents which declared my father was of sound mind. Smiling hopelessly at a nurse I said, 'This is my dad!" She laughed in response and recounted how at night, once all the patients were settled and a reasonable calm had settled over the geriatric ward, a sudden riotous burst of zoo and barnyard noises would erupt from his room. The repertoire was extensive, an acoustically accurate rendition of various domestic and exotic creatures. Even in my middle age, I found I was still able to experience the same flushes of extreme embarrassment I had known so well in my youth about something my father had done.

With the power of attorney documentation completed as best possible, I began to query my father about various points of his affairs. I had surmised from a cursory inspection of the heaped-up mail that he had amassed a huge credit card debt, and there was also a considerable amount of overdue income tax. Now I learned that there was no will, no life insurance and no way of knowing what the total extent of debts and assets were. There was certainly not enough cash on hand to hire a lawyer to help me muddle through it all. I was on my own, holding the proverbial bag.

I was able to meet with my father's doctor, who had initially contacted me about the situation. He expressed deep gratitude that I had come to look after my father's affairs and that there was someone he could consult in regard to decisions about treatment and care. We reviewed my father's medical and social history. Dad had been seeing an associate of this doctor, a woman who refused to see him when he became too aggressive toward her with his usual strange sexual innuendos. The doctor explained that dad had become an infamous local personality. Those who knew him either loved or despised him. Knowing his various personalities, I understood all too well.

The doctor explained that it was possible to operate on the brain tumour but there was little point. My father's general condition included prostate problems, angina, diabetes and deteriorating mental health. Dad had little hope of leading a reasonable life even without the tumour. This doctor was a gracious man and gave me plenty of time to discuss all aspects of the situation. It was concluded that the best care was to minimize pain and discomfort, allowing nature to take its course and affording dignity to everyone, especially my father.

The morning rushed by. There was so much to deal with that I did not know where to start. I had to go to the Toronto airport later and meet my relatives arriving from England. I had time to organize father's finances; that was a small enough chore as he had none. I settled some accounts with an insurance company and sorted through a small mountain of mail that remained after a preliminary culling. I eliminated all but the latest letters from creditors, the pension administrators and Revenue Canada. There was still a heap of correspondence.

With a little time yet before I had to leave for the airport, I drove to the funeral home to make arrangements. In preparation for when the time came, I wanted to pre-arrange a simple cremation and the provision of death certificates that I would need to deal with the creditors. It seemed morbid and callous to be doing this when the man was still alive, but it must be done while I was there. Sorting it all out from over two thousand miles away after my father had died would be yet another nightmare. I discussed it all with my father that morning. He had delivered mail for several years to a particular funeral home and had made friends with the proprietor. Now he wanted 'Rudy to look after things, he's a good man.'

I was used to dealing with death. I had seen friend's lives end violently before my eyes and other people have died in my arms. I have seen my share of carnage and am resolved that dead is dead. Close friends and relatives had passed away throughout my life but I had never before set foot in a funeral home. I did not know what to expect. Entering through a back door, I found myself inside a cavernous building. A long, richly carpeted hall ran between two sumptuously decorated rooms that would make ideal banquet halls. The building had a certain hushed, elegant austerity and did not seem at all morbid. I had vaguely expected bodies in caskets, gently weeping people, haunting organ music, a coffin showroom and possibly a faint odour of formaldehyde. There was none of that. In fact, the entire building seemed to be uninhabited. 'Hello?' I called and then again, a bit louder. No answer. Again and again I called until finally a young man appeared, climbing the stairs from the basement. 'Busy down in the workshop', I mused.

Thoughtlessly I greeted the fellow who was dressed in a dapper pin-striped suit by saying, 'Ah finally, a live one!' Like father, like son I suppose. I do have a knack for uttering the inappropriate. Everything was soon settled. It was amazingly matter-of-fact and straightforward. Yes, no, no, yes; questions were asked and answered; forms were completed; it could not have been simpler. The ostentatious decor clearly showed that other people spent considerably more to dispatch their loved ones. This however, was death on a budget and I was dealing with things in the manner that my father wished. It is clearly an advantage to do this sort of thing when not overwhelmed with the despair of an unexpected exodus. I wrote a cheque and was on my way well within the time I had allotted myself. 'Next please', I thought, smiling grimly. The largest item was now off my agenda and I felt that I had already accomplished more than enough for one day. I headed for the airport with a little time to spare.

Toronto airport, now renamed Pearson, has become a monstrous, sprawling entity of several terminals, massive parking facilities and other amenities related to international and continental air travel. The flight that I was to meet was arriving at the original new terminal, built when the airport had officially been established as an important facility for global flights in the mid nineteen-sixties. Commercial jet aircraft were becoming a practical reality and the masses were flocking into the skies. As a boy riding his bicycle, it took me hours to pass through rural countryside before finally arriving at the former air force base at Malton. As I neared the airport

I would pass the severed wings of a jet fighter. They were raised to form an inverted V for a gateway to an auto wrecker's. The A. V. Roe aircraft factory was immediately across the road; I mused that perhaps the wings had been salvaged from the infamous Arrow. Once an entire squadron of Dehavilland Chipmunk trainers had been refurbished and then made surplus by the airforce. They sat at Malton airport for months and were finally sold off for fifteen hundred dollars apiece. At the time I remember scheming of a way to raise that lofty sum but it may as well have been a million dollars.

Little was recognizable. This former ultimate terminal building had once been a prominent landmark for miles around. Now it was lost within a maze of terminals and hangars. There were no working farms within miles of the airport, which now seemed virtually downtown in the megalopolis that Toronto had become. There was once huge scepticism about why the airport was located so far from the city. A multi-layered car park was built on top of the terminal building and I drove as far into the upper levels as I could. The top level was barricaded against entry because of restoration work, but I climbed over the fence and walked to the guard rail at the edge. I looked down on the tarmac below where several aircraft were parked. Further in the distance I could see the active runway and the incredible number of flights that continuously arrived and departed. Air Canada handled an average of over twelve flights per hour, or one every five minutes. Suddenly time rolled back thirty years to the few occasions when my father would bring me to this same spot. We came for the pleasure of plane spotting! We had not done it regularly, and until this moment I had entirely forgotten about those hours simply watching aircraft. It was something my father and I had done together, actually sharing a mutual enjoyment! This now crumbling structure had then been recently completed and its height afforded a vast panoramic view. On a clear day you could see out past the lakeshore several miles to the south. By watching diligently, you could see aircraft approaching long before they crossed the runway threshold.

I always thrill to the sound of aircraft propellers and the resonant whine of jet engines. The smell of jet exhaust is a heady perfume to me and, as it wafted up, I instantly recalled this same vista thirty years ago. Aircraft were not boarded then via weather-proof corridors that extended tightly against the fuselage. Passengers walked to the bottom of mobile wheeled stairs and stood out in the weather waiting their turn to ascend into the aircraft. Turbo-prop aircraft like the Britannia and Trans Canada Airline's Viscount and Vanguard were fascinating new technology.

Piston-engine propelled aircraft were still state of the art then, and the start-up procedure was always a fascinating ritual. DC threes, fours, sixes and sevens were the popular airplanes of the day. Constellations and Northstars were exotic long distance sky ships. When the last passengers had boarded and the aircraft doors closed, the wheeled stairways were removed as the last of the baggage was loaded. Ground crew in white coveralls took their positions around the aircraft. Some leaned into the massive propeller blades and slowly walked them around a few times in order to rotate the engines, lubricating their internal parts. Various men were stationed in strategic positions with fire extinguishers. Others manned a ground power unit, or GPU, that was plugged into the fuselage. Finally a signalman strolled into position where he could see all four engines as well as the captain sitting in the cockpit. He would pause like a conductor before his orchestra. Then, raising one baton, he pointed it at the first engine while vigorously twirling a second baton, the signal to start it up. Nothing would happen for several breath-holding seconds. Ponderously, the propeller would begin to rotate slowly and then stop again. Nothing happened as the inertial starters were re-energized. Again they would begin to revolve slowly. Ignitions were turned on and, with a mighty, clattering roar and a huge cloud of smoke from the exhaust the propeller would stutter then accelerate into a whirling blur. The process was repeated three more times until all engines were snarling with eagerness as they warmed to operating temperature. Finally the captain would give the signalman a thumbs-up. The GPU was disconnected and driven out of the way and the wheel chocks were waved away. The engines revved to a higher note as the propeller pitch was set to fine and then the aircraft began to creep forward, turning away from the terminal building.

It seemed to take a very long time until the plane had taxied to the far downwind end of the runway. The flight crew had performed myriad checks and tests and then rolled it into position on the runway. Engines would be advanced to a screaming crescendo before the brakes were released and the huge polished aluminium ship slowly began to trundle along the runway. Flight at first appeared to be hopeless, but eventually with a stately, throbbing drone the behemoth plane would raise its nose and ponderously waddle into flight like an overfed goose. Airline ads promised comfortable overnight berths and it was incredible that people could travel to Europe in only twenty-four hours. Jet-powered DC eights and 707s displaced the piston-engine aircraft and air travel was revolutionized forever. It was suddenly possible for aircraft to carry hundreds of passengers non-stop to destinations anywhere on the planet. In a few more years jumbo jets displaced the earlier jets. Masses of people now cavalierly travel anywhere on the planet without consideration of risk or delay. Less than one hundred years ago, a powered flight had not yet occurred!

While on these plane-watching excursions, my father would always remind me about a photograph taken when I was two years old. I was dressed in a toddler's winter suit, standing in a snowy setting and pointing up at the sky. Dad always jovially claimed that I was watching vampire jet fighters of the RCAF fly past and I would shout: 'Pet pane, pet pane'. It was corny and pathetic that these visits to the airport were a highlight of my youth, but it was a good solid, warm memory. That was worth a lot.

I descended into the grey bowels of the terminal to meet my uncle's flight. Thankfully, the overhead monitors showed a delay of only minutes. The arrival area was crowded with the usual mob of impatient, rude, frustrated people and their whining children. I hate crowds. In fact, I have a distinct phobia of them. Standing with my back to a wall, I surveyed the scene, fighting to remain placid. 'Oh well, a few more minutes and I'll have a new set of problems, uncle Henry and cousin Clarissa', I mused to myself, focusing away from my panic that always rises in a swirling rabble.

I had met this uncle when he had previously brought his family to the west coast to visit my sister and me. They were not sophisticated people, but pleasant and earthy, taking delight in the smallest things and the company of extended family. Uncle Henry in fact was rather gormless, 'A British hillbilly' I called him, but it was a term of endearment for my father's brother and I was delighted to see him again. He was ebullient and common but also warm and caring, the key to a sense of family that my father had for some reason worked diligently to undo. Cousin Clarissa was another matter, a mysterious enigma. My father claimed special closeness between himself and this woman, but I did not understand their relationship.

Bedraggled, disoriented, weary-looking people trickled through the customs and immigration gate. My party was nearly last to emerge. Attired in his usual tweed sport jacket underneath a short raincoat, Henry emerged with a toothy smile that split his face from ear to large wiggling ear.

He has a goofy appeal that I cannot resist. Cousin Clarissa brought up the rear looking peevish and demure. Their baggage had all arrived intact and soon we were on their way to Oakville.

Both travellers were exhausted from their flight and desperately needed to rest. True to my father's description and Henry's warnings, Clarissa was a fiddling sort of person who took an eternity to do the simplest things and arrive at decisions. It was no small task to finally find agreeable accommodation in a small local hotel and the day was well worn by the time they settled into their rooms. Clarissa was a frustrating person to deal with. No amount of urging could induce her to expedite her progress. In fact, she seemed to slow even more in response to any sort of prompting. Henry decided it would be best if they rested for the night, and waited until the next morning to see his brother. I felt used-up, dazed, and ready to collapse. I had set myself a gruelling pace and wondered how I would survive the next few days. I readily agreed to leave the two to their own devices for the evening and, much relieved, retired to my father's apartment via a liquor store on the way. It was obvious that I would need constant fuel additives for the duration of this ordeal.

Shattered as I felt, I was unable to relax and decided to sort out my father's belongings. Earlier that day I had discussed my agenda with the doctor and explained about the apartment. I asked what should be done with my father's personal effects. The doctor assured me repeatedly that there was no way that dad would ever recover. He was terminally ill and would never again require clothing or personal items. There was still a fetid smell to the apartment and I set to the task of bagging the clothing in the closets and drawers for the dumpster. The full realization of what I was doing hit me as I began to put my father's shoes into a large orange garbage bag. I broke down and began to sob. Weeping openly, I sat on the floor and let my anguish gush out. It was those damned shoes that had triggered the reaction. My father had massive bunions on both feet and all his shoes were unmistakably deformed, uniquely his. As a boy I used to polish his shoes; it was one of my chores. I recalled the walking boots used on the postal routes, the gardening shoes and the Sunday shoes with their soft, comfortable leather and thick crepe soles. Now I was throwing out a living man's clothing. I felt as if I was taking a hand in confirming my own father's fate. It was nonsense to feel this way, I knew. There was so much to be done and this was just one more task, yet it did not seem at all right. The last time I had felt this way was when I had been asked to shoot a friend's old and ailing dog, ending its misery and affording it a dignified demise. It was an act of love, but a sickening, bitter experience. I felt the same now.

I next tackled the massive collection of video tapes, books and magazines. The videos represented the twisted personality that haunted my father. A large number of the tapes dealt with railways and steam locomotives. These I knew were expensive, and most were apparently not yet paid for. I had noted the purchases on numerous different credit card statements. None of those accounts had seen even a minimum payment for a very long time. Other videos dealt with birds and wildlife, military bands, famous British architecture, successful Christian living, life in nudist colonies and a few pornographic films, all on one shelf. This was the conundrum that was my father's style - bizarre eclecticism. One never quite knew from which angle he was approaching life at any given moment. He had always seemed torn between a quest for righteousness and a compulsion for his notion of the iniquitous. The man's single constant was his perpetual inconsistency.

I finally divided his possessions into four categories. One was junk, things that were essentially worthless to anyone and easily discarded. Then there were things of enough worth, usually sentimental or legal, that would be shipped at great expense to my home for further evaluation and distribution between my brother and sister. Some of the furniture, appliances, and his vehicle were of value to his second wife or the apartment manager who had been especially helpful. He deserved a significant token of appreciation. Anything left over would go to the Salvation Army. It was as fair and generous a solution as I could determine under the circumstances. As there was little of huge monetary value, I would not have to wrangle with anyone about the division of goods. There was not much to show for an entire lifetime, especially with the massive debts that this seventy-three year old man had accumulated once again.

After another nearly sleepless night, I went to a restaurant on the main street that opened early and ate a hearty breakfast. I dined at the same place each morning, and already felt like old friends with the matronly waitress there. I was repeatedly delighted and surprised at how friendly and helpful were most people in my old hometown. Perhaps, in my present state of duress, I was emitting some signal that solicited this response but I suspected that most people here were naturally amiable and I had simply forgotten, or never known this. I basked in the warm feeling it gave me, and later realized how that aura of well-being had helped sustain me throughout the ordeal.

Everywhere I went I found myself looking into faces, to see if they were someone I recognized, or if they might recognize me. After more than a quarter century, obviously no one was going to look the same. It seemed inevitable someone was left from the time when this had been my home and I went through the telephone book, looking up names that I could remember. I found several, but each evening I was too exhausted to pursue anything beyond my current obligations. I saw only one woman who appeared to have been a former classmate. We shared a brief smile of familiarity but each of us hurried on our way without looking back, both in too much of a hurry to risk the time required for conversation.

After breakfast I went to my uncle's hotel. Henry had been up for hours, having taken a long walk and made himself breakfast in his hotel room. Clarissa was still in her waking mode and would be for the next few hours. Henry and I sat drinking coffee and discussing my father's situation and affairs. I reviewed all that the doctor had told me and also what had transpired since I had first arrived. Ever since I could remember, there had always been a rift between my father and Henry. There was a third brother, Adam, who had been institutionalized most of his life. I often wondered if there was not a common genetic flaw shared between Adam and my father. I knew little of my family's history. Dad had offered only vague, inconsistent accounts that did not make any sense. Little made sense. I was confused and doubtful about anything I was told. I always felt a little guilty, and suspicious of my understanding of our origins. I longed for a solid sense of who I and my family really were.

A few years previously, Henry had undertaken the daunting task of compiling a family history, complete with copies of every old family photo available and extensive family trees as far back, and in every direction as possible. I am forever grateful for this, as it has enabled me to feel a sense of heritage that I had never had before. Now I inquired about what had come between my father and his brother Roger. Henry was not certain, saying he suspected that dad had been jealous of Roger and his closeness to their parents. He pointed out that my father, the oldest son, had abandoned the family, emigrating to Canada as soon as possible after the war. Of the three brothers, Henry had been left to look after the family farm when my grandfather suffered a stroke and became bed-ridden for the rest of his life. Henry and his wife had cared for my ailing grand parents while busy raising their own children. Apparently my grandmother had been fiercely matriarchal and increasingly cantankerous as she aged and after grandfather was incapacitated. My father had refused to show any interest in becoming involved, and eventually accused Henry and their mother of plotting against him.

There had been a huge rift between dad and his parents, especially with my grandfather. It had culminated when he was twenty-one years old and his father had allegedly beaten him mercilessly. I had heard the story several times and now Henry confirmed it He was quick to point out that my grandfather had not been a violent man and the attack was quite out of character. Although there was no clear recollection of what provoked the incident, it apparently had something to do with a girlfriend of my father. Certainly it had been a crucial turning point in his life. Shortly after, he had left home and come to Canada. Henry had come to Canada in order to vindicate himself of his brother's suspicion and animosity. It was time to throw aside blame and bury the hatchet, no matter who was at fault for the long years of estrangement. When I first learned that Henry was coming to visit, I told my father, who immediately flew into a rage. He adamantly declared that he wanted nothing to do with his brother, and only softened when he learned that Clarissa was also coming. I was desperately curious to learn about the bond between my father and Clarissa and insisted that Henry explain.

During the war, when German air raids began to devastate the Cities of England, British children were evacuated to rural areas. Clarissa lived in Putney, a suburb of London, and it was logical that she spend the duration of the war with her relatives on their farm in the Midlands. Dad had been fourteen when war broke out and Clarissa a few years younger. He had been attending an art school in Coventry at the time and was showing great promise with an outstanding artistic talent. Ironically, in consideration of why Clarissa had come to the farm, she probably endured more of the Blitzkrieg in Coventry than she would have in her own home. Coventry was the heart of England's industrialization and became the city most heavily bombed by the Luftwaffe. My father's school was soon levelled. As if that was not bad enough, the RAF constructed a mock aerodrome only a mile from the family farm. It was a constantly targeted decoy for bomber and night fighter attacks.

The stories were horrific. Night after night the family cowered in a shelter on the lawn as stray bombs rained down, explosions rocking the earth for miles around. One night an incendiary bomb and its parachute had landed on the roof of the house, not igniting, and rolled down into the rain gutter where it stayed unexploded until a retrieval crew eventually arrived. Their farm was littered at times with bits of debris from bombers shot out of the sky. There was a story of German air charts scattered throughout the garden. A hired hand on a neighbouring farm had been ploughing a field when a low-flying German fighter plane had strafed and killed his team of horses. Everyone knew someone killed in the raids.

Throughout those years, my grandfather donned his overcoat every morning and placidly bicycled twelve miles to his job at the Hawker-Siddley aircraft plant in the city. He worked as a master craftsman with the title of 'Jig and Body Maker'. The family later learned he was part of a team working with Frank Whittle, desperately prototyping a jet fighter aircraft for the RAF. He returned to the farm each evening and worked it as best he could. It was a bizarre time of extremes, tof he incongruous and unimaginable, of unspeakable brutality, unfathomable endurance, sacrifice and caring for each other. I had seen a photograph of my grandfather astride his bicycle on his way to work, attired in his overcoat and tweed cap, three-piece suit and tie. His round, wire-rim spectacles gleamed in the morning sun, a

Home Guard Lee Enfield .303 rifle and lunch-pail strapped over his shoulder, an implacable grin on his face. This image seemed strange to me, but it was the way people lived and endured the war.

It was a time when everyone, in their own way, lived each day to its fullest because they were constantly confronted with their mortality. Each moment could be their last. The British civilian endured hardship with stoic, cheerful, quiet determination. Severe rationing was in effect; hoarding was considered a heinous offence. I could only imagine what closeness had developed between my father and his cousin Clarissa in those circumstances, but at least now I understood a little better. I reasoned there was little that anyone could do that was unforgivable when living under such duress, so long as it was not at someone else's expense.

Now it was time for these final remnants of the family who had shared those times so long ago to be reunited for one last time. I drove Henry and Clarissa to the hospital and showed them to father's bedside. Greeting him as usual, I went through the daily ritual of helping him decide on his menu for the following day. Allowing the two new visitors to stand silently by gave them a chance to observe dad's state of mind and his general condition, so that they better understood how to deal with him. Finally I announced his guests and motioned to Henry and Clarissa to each say hello. It was a poignant moment. Everyone burst into tears at once. I stepped to the side of the room and let the magic of the moment work its course. My own face was leaking too!

Once the flood of tears had abated and their conversation had begun to flow easily, I left them together and went off to tend to other business. Henry and Clarissa later walked back to their hotel and telephoned me at my father's apartment where I was still sorting through things. They had endured a long, exhausting day and were going to retire for the night. I met them again in the morning and reviewed their previous day's visit. I learned happily that all had gone well. Henry felt that he had resolved the differences between himself and his brother and was visibly more at ease than on the previous day. Clarissa was subdued as usual but indicated that she was glad that she had come.

They had arranged seats on a flight returning to Britain late in the evening. Henry thought they should go and visit dad for a while in the morning, before taking the afternoon to compose themselves and rest before returning to the airport. It would be a hard morning, knowing it was a final good bye; everyone lingered over breakfast delaying the inevitable as long as possible. Finally it was time to go. We soon found ourselves again at my father's bedside. He was in good spirits and delighted that everyone was there. Soon he startled Henry and Clarissa with a question about someone named Lily. They were both obviously taken back by the question, looking sharply at each other. I realized that I was about to learn something important.

'Who?' responded Henry, 'Lily, Lily Powers', my father inquired. 'Have you kept in touch with her?' For a moment Henry was lost for words: 'No, David, how could we? It's been over fifty years.' My father was silent for a long while after muttering something about a boy, the pause pregnant with innuendo, but suddenly he changed the subject and began talking about a fish that he had once caught. Amazed at that recollection, Henry confirmed the story. There had been a locally famous pike in a small lake several miles from the family farm. This huge fish had become a legend, and was occasionally seen lying in shallow reed beds around the edges of the lake. It was a local challenge to try and catch the old pike but no-one ever had a bit of luck, until one day dad simply caught and landed the beast. The only way he could transport the huge fish home was by tying it across the handlebars of his bicycle. The boy had proudly pedalled his way home through two small villages. Apparently there had been a photograph of young David grinning wildly as he held his bike with the pike hanging down from either end of the handlebars. I had never heard this story before so I knew it had been long forgotten. It was a delightful tale that had everyone laughing and eased the tension somewhat as the time drew near for Henry and Clarissa to say their final farewell to my father.

Tears and prayers flowed freely. I recognized the value of prayer in this situation and although I recoil from anything religious, I knew that here, for these people, it was an essential component in dealing with their distress. The rest of that hour was a blur with sobbing, hugging, soft words and the heaviness of knowing that one is saying good-bye for the final time to someone who was still alive. I sagged a little more when I realized that I would have to go through this again with my father, alone.

Outside the hospital it was a sunny spring day, fine and cool, but with a promise in the air of a warm afternoon. I took Henry and Clarissa to lunch at a restaurant with a patio and we sat in the fresh air and sunlight trying to encapsulate the morning and salvage the remains of the day. I was brimming with questions about Lily Powers. At first, Henry was reluctant to discuss much but I insisted. It seemed that this person might well be the key to whatever it was that had haunted my father for most of his life. Finally Henry began to explain.

'Lily Powers lived on the farm across the road'. Henry spoke slowly, pausing while he chose his words carefully. 'It was a dairy farm, quite a successful one too, which had been in the family for several generations and was well established. When war broke out, Lily was a young woman, probably in her mid to late teens, very pretty and well liked by everyone who knew her. She delivered milk to

Coventry with a pony cart, making her daily rounds and selling it by the ladle from the metal milk cans on the cart'. I expressed surprise that a girl would be charged with such a responsibility and was exposed to such risk in a war-ravished city. Henry pointed out that with everyone contributing to the war as best they could. Some had to assume duties they would never have otherwise considered. 'Anyway,' Henry continued, 'The art school your father had been attending had been bombed flat during one of the first raids on Coventry, so he stayed home, working the family farm and helped at the Powers farm across the road. Over time, He and Lily became very close. Our father thought they were too close, and he tried to interfere and keep them apart. I suspect that the big row they had was something to do with Lily because we learned soon after that she was pregnant.'

'During the war there was a tremendous shortage of manpower and some of the more placid and trustworthy prisoners of war were being pressed into service on farms. An Italian POW was sent to the Powers farm to work as a labourer. He used to wear a bright orange pair of coveralls with the large letters POW displayed across the back. Once everyone learned that Lily was in the family way, it was generally concluded that the Italian fellow had been the father of her little boy. Today your father asked what had become of his son, meaning his and Lily's, and it's got me thinking I can tell you! Perhaps that's where the problem has lain all these years. He once mentioned that he was expecting someone from the U.K. to join him as soon as he was established in Canada and that they never did. Perhaps it was Lily. With your father, as you know, you could never be sure of anything he said but now maybe, some of it makes sense.'

It was a powerful discovery for me. I thought of all the times my father had stood staring out a window, gnawing at his fingernails until they bled. There was a distant look in his eyes, and I had thought my father was reliving some indelible wartime memory. As it turned out he was, but there was more to it than just bombs whistling down again and again. Perhaps he was grieving a lost love, a lost child, a lost life. My father had met my own mother in a boarding house where they lived in Milton, then a small town to the north of Oakville. Was it what people called a rebound romance? Had my father married my mother in an effort to obliterate the pain of losing the one he truly loved and always would? Did I have an older half-brother living somewhere in England? There were so many questions, old and new, that could now never be answered.

After lunch, Henry indicated that they would prefer to see some of the local area, find a little distraction from the intensity of the morning and clear their minds a bit before the flight home. I drove them around town, showing them some of the grand old colonial homes and places where interesting incidents had occurred during my childhood. Since there was plenty of time to kill, and to satisfy my own curiosity, I drove to the east end of the county to try and find the last farm where my family had lived before moving to town. It was difficult, groping for recognizable landmarks, all the while immersed in conversation with Henry, while Clarissa lurked silently in the back seat.

When I was a child, the road was a narrow country lane called the County Line, or the First Line. Fortunately I recognized a stately old home and realized the road was now a broad avenue called Churchill Boulevard. My hope of finding the place fell, but I drove on in what I hoped was the right direction. The road narrowed. Then suddenly, appearing as it always had behind a rise in a hill, was the house. It was a two-storey brick house that had been renovated and painted, but it was the same house without a doubt. There was the long, sloping front lawn where I had played as a four-year-old down by the tractor shed. I used to play there alone in the dusky late autumn afternoons. A flood of smells came to mind. The air was cold, crisp and fresh, with a perfume of fallen leaves, fresh apples, pears and pumpkins stored in the barn next to the shed. I remembered the aroma of the tractor shed - that curious sweet reek of grease, gasoline and bits of drying vegetation clinging to the machinery. Then there was wood smoke, the sweet, tangy, heady perfume that sings out home, comfort, food, warmth, security. To this day, I always feel pangs of hunger whenever I smell wood smoke; it is linked to my childhood on that lawn. The falling darkness came with tingling cold on my face, hands, and toes, and with that smoke aroma. Then there came light and warmth on entering the house, the cosy ambience of the kitchen and a simple meal simmering on the wood cook stove. Supper time with a chance of a beating!

The house was now enclosed, but when I was a child a long, open wooden porch ran across the front of the house. I would clump noisily up the wooden steps to the door leading into the mud room. From there, one door opened into the kitchen and one opened over a set of steep stairs descending into the basement. I would remove my coat and boots and then enter the kitchen. One evening as I struggled with my boots, I leaned against the basement door. It swung open and I tumbled backwards down the stairs into the dark basement. I was not seriously injured, only bruised, but I recall the detached terror I felt as I clunked over and over down the stairs into the dark, dank basemen, and the crashing stop that knocked me breathless. I lay on the cold floor, ears roaring, stars dancing in my head. I knew that, when people died, they stopped breathing. Since I could not draw a breath, I lay there with a desperate strangled feeling, believing that I was dead. I waited for the angels. They did not arrive. Mother was screeching at me from the doorway above and sadly, I conceded that yet I lived I can still see her dark silhouette at the top of the stairs, her voice a mixture of fear and anger, as if I had deliberately flung myself down the stairs.

The basement, that fucking basement! I had other memories of it too. Its primary function was to house a huge, wheezing wood furnace. There was a chute from outside where you put the firewood into a huge pile beneath in the basement. I mused that it was the classic old woodpile story, but it was true and certainly not at all humorous. The slivery kindling and my bare bottom often met by that woodpile, a never-ending saga of corporal punishment for the simple sake of doing it. My parents clearly felt that spankings and beatings were an essential component of child rearing, like cod-liver oil, having to eat all my over-cooked vegetables and wear too many clothes. It was always 'for your own good'. How screwing up my mind for the rest of my life was for my own good is a hopeless mystery. Once again I realized I was choking back bitter anger for a childhood eternally punctuated with misery. But the basement held a happy memory as well and I grasped it fiercely, relating the story to Clarissa and Henry.

I had been given a cardboard box filled with board-ends, a tin can full of used nails, an old hammer with one claw broken off, and a small, rusty saw. I sawed at the boards with difficulty, hampered by my childish awkwardness. The saw often skipped; I cut my hands with the dull blade regularly. The nails all had to be straightened, and I smashed my fingers repeatedly, a searing agony. Often I split the boards when I drove the nails in, but I persevered. I cannot remember ever actually building anything significant, but I know this was where my creativity and passion for building things had taken root. It was probably one of the most positive and formative things my parents ever did for me . An innocent act at the time, probably to keep me amused and out of their way, but it was where I began to develop skills in that basement which I would use to good advantage all my life.

At the front corner of the house was another small porch where I often played. There were no other children in the area and I was always alone, so I invented imaginary characters and exotic adventures to amuse myself. Still standing by the porch was a large cedar tree; I could remember collecting its seeds, pretending they were tiny bananas. I saw myself again loading the seeds into a toy truck and a little boat that I had acquired. I could even smell them again and taste the acrid tang when I put them in my mouth, their resin sticky on my dirty hands. Perhaps the memory was inspired by the rotted remains of an old wooden wagon wheel that lay in the bushes by the side of the driveway. The wheel was in exactly the same spot where it sat nearly forty years before. It used to be painted white with a bright red hub, a landmark so that visitors would know when they had found the right driveway.

Red hubs! Another memory raced through my mind. Dad still owned the 1938 Ford then, and I remembered its red wheels again, a small chrome hubcap in the centre of each with the red letters V8 and small semi-circular holes around the edge of the rim. I had my little wooden wagon then; it too had red wheels with similar tiny holes in them and I used to ride in the wagon there, rolling it down the bumpy driveway that ran around the edge of the lawn. I wondered what had happened to that wagon, once a big part of my life.

On the same corner of the house, a window looked out from each corner down onto the porch roof and the front lawn. I remembered all the hours spent looking out from those windows. Torpid June evenings, far too hot to sleep, I would lie on my bed listening to the big, brown June beetles thumping against the screens and all the night sounds outside in the surrounding fields. Summer nights were hot, terribly humid, and airless - or close, as some people said. Such a night would be spent lying in sweat-damp sheets listening to the building rumble of a thunderstorm out over Lake Ontario, hoping it would come ashore and bring the relief of rain. Sometimes it did, crashing and flashing wonderfully, passing too quickly, rumbling off into the sticky darkness, thundering in the distance like a passing train, often leaving the air even more damp and fetid than before.

Other times I was horribly ill, confined to bed in that room for interminable periods, my mother spoon-feeding me gruel and chicken broth. Often she worked late into the evening in the next room, the rattle of her Singer treadle sewing machine clattering incessantly on, making sleep even more impossible. This was the house where my sister must have been conceived; I wondered if my mother had been making clothes for the expected baby. I remembered a smiling sewing machine salesman and a new Elna electric sewing machine, the whirring sound and its variable speed controlled by a massive foot switch. In a fit of madness after mother had left him years later, my father accused her of conceiving my sister with the salesman, a story he insisted on repeating annoyingly despite my fierce sarcasm. Typical of the old bastard, I thought, so carelessly disenfranchising his own children on a silly, invented whim that was of no advantage, even to himself. I took some photographs of the house, its occupants curious but reluctant to challenge my boldness. 'Sorry, folks, for being rude', I thought ruefully, 'But I was here first and I may not be back again for a while.'

I drove Henry and Clarissa back to town where we had dinner, accompanied by the usual sort of conversation between people that are about to be separated by long distance and time. I had never travelled to Britain, so there were promises of sights to see and good times when I finally did go. However, any thought of what may lie in the distant future seemed hollow to me when I had so much to deal with immediately. I was already reviewing what I yet had to do that day. As I drove Henry and Clarissa to meet an express bus to the airport, I was thinking, 'This whole trip is about nothing but damned good byes.' They waved to me from inside the tinted windows. Then they were gone. I was on my own again, relieved but exhausted, shattered, and feeling utterly alone.

Throughout the few previous, hectic days of their visit I had stolen whatever time I could to slowly organize the details of putting father's affairs in order. Now I could manage their completion after returning home to British Columbia. I even managed to find a little time to spend at the local library, researching a few events from my past that held special interest for me. I was looking for information on the yacht 'Mir'. In addition, I photocopied several newspaper pages from the library's microfiche files. Bread was advertised for sixteen cents a loaf, new cars were twenty five hundred dollars, a house could be bought for ten thousand dollars. An article described the ultimate new luxury car soon to be produced at the local Ford plant, the Edsel. Unfortunately, the story said, the car would be priced too high for many, selling for over thirty-five hundred dollars.

My week in Oakville was wearing on. I had met some interesting people, gathered valuable information and finished all the pertinent business at hand. All that was left was the final exit from the apartment and disposing of father's old vehicle.

Dad's second wife was, in politically popular vernacular, learning disabled, which is what attracted him to her; she was someone he could control absolutely. He had made her sorry life a total misery. If it had not been for a large family network to council her and keep my father aware that they disapproved of the marriage and were watching him, chances were that this tragic situation would have had an even uglier outcome.

There were two children by this second marriage. The first was a boy, eighteen years younger than me. He had left home at the age of fifteen for similar reasons as I had at age thirteen. When I reunited with my brother after twenty years, we both agreed that it seemed dad was often jealous of us and had done his best to keep us alienated from each other. It was interesting for us to both note that dad had a way of trying to cancel events or activities that we looked forward to, usually just before they took place. School trips, family outings, virtually anything that was worth anticipating would be cruelly and coldly countermanded. It seemed to be our father's way of proving to himself that he had some control, and affording him an opportunity for antagonism, including perhaps a fight or a beating, and more proof to himself of his power. We also compared notes on his incongruous behaviour and how he had a way of utterly embarrassing us. I recounted his habit, when around small children, of suddenly bulging his eyes at them, extending his false teeth out of his mouth and vigorously rattling them. He thought he was uproariously funny, but the children were invariably terrified and other adults disgusted. My brother told me about a church they had attended which was a posh, stuffy, upper-crust Baptist congregation. One day in the crowded foyer, Dad plucked a hair from his nose and loudly began speculating about why nose hairs were curly and rough! We had both attended this church at different times and learned that we had each had to wear ugly polyester suits and similar hideous shoes. The fact that we had endured similar humiliations formed a strong common bond between us.

Despite a tumultuous childhood, my brother Ryan had proven to be a brilliant young man and an achiever. As a teenager, he had toured Europe as a talented musician. By the time he was in his mid-twenties, he had explored several career opportunities and chosen a solid career as an airline pilot. The other child, my half-sister, was severely retarded, and would remain entirely dependent on her mother for her whole life. That was a situation that I soon perceived I should leave well alone.

Mother and daughter, Helen and Susan, lived in the same old rented house, trying to maintain it as best they could on their own with limited resources. Forbidden by a court restraining order from going near the premises, the best dad had been able to do was rent the apartment overlooking the yard, in order to watch their comings and goings. He had been charged with sexually abusing Susan. Although the evidence was inconclusive, he was fined and prevented from being near the house and garden that were his reason for being. A divorce followed, much to the final relief of all the family that had despaired over the eventual outcome of this unseemly marriage. Although the old man vehemently denied having done anything wrong, everyone who knew him was well aware of his incessant inappropriate behaviour. He became an outcast, an object of ridicule and contempt. The only friends he may have had left were new ones who didn't know the rest of the story.

I felt sorry for the two women, but was unsure what I could do for them. I did not know them well, having already left home by the time of my father's second marriage. My father had made it clear to me that I was now considered at best a nuisance. I was disgusted that my father had developed a relationship of any sort with someone who was so clearly handicapped. Helen possessed no apparent attributes. She was neither attractive nor self sufficient in any way. She shuffled about in an almost ape-like way, her speech stilted, her vocabulary limited. She seemed resolved to serve my father's whims like a trained animal. I had deliberately distanced myself from the entire situation for almost thirty years.

Because of my new-found relationship with Ryan, the half brother from that marriage, my opinion of his mother had mellowed. In fact I felt guilty about my previous contempt, finally understanding that she had also been victimized horribly by my father, used and abused like so many others in his life. I arranged for Helen to visit dad's apartment in the company of one of her brothers and select any appliances and furniture that she wanted. There was no life insurance forthcoming and no way that I could offer her money that did not exist. Helen and Susan existed on social assistance, which left little money for anything extra. Helen's family had been urging her to find an apartment and move away from the crumbling old house that was such a burden to live in. But because they already had a roof over their head, there was little that Social Services would do to help Helen and Susan with moving expenses.

The only thing that I could think of, which would also help me solve another problem, was to let Helen have whatever proceeds came from the sale of my father's vehicle. Typically, the old man had added various multicoloured paint accents, strange bumper stickers, extra lights, vents, mirrors and silly horns until the once sedate truck looked hideous. It had little resale value, and it reminded me of all the old trucks and vans that he had owned when I was a boy. Dad had managed to turn every vehicle into a grotesque embarrassment. I did not know what to do with the vehicle. Being short on both time and patience, I was eager for a simple solution. I arranged that one of Helen's brothers would buy it for a pittance of five hundred dollars, payable to Helen. The brother later reneged on his agreement and I was furious that a brother would do that to his sister. The bullshit never ended! The money was to help her with the expense of moving to a nearby apartment. It wasn't much, but just enough to make the move a possibility. Helen was resourceful, however, and later managed to sell it for the same price to another relative in time to complete her move. She was elated and very thankful that leaving the old place had become possible.

Helen insisted that I come for dinner and I agreed on the understanding that I would not be able to stay for long because of all the little things yet left to do. Actually, I was exhausted and just wanted to rest. It was a strange experience to drive up to my old home from so many years ago. I felt like a stranger and yet it seemed as if I had only been away a day. The last time that I had set foot on this property was in mid-winter. I had returned from a disastrous trip to British Columbia when I was eighteen years old. Out of work, desperately broke, cold, hungry, entirely alone and with no place to go, I had come to my father's house as a last resort. I had not been home or seen my father in over two years, having travelled extensively back and forth across the country. I thought that my father would be at least a little interested in seeing me. I had hitch-hiked home through bitter winter weather with no money and little to eat. I had been forced to rely on the charity of strangers to survive and was down to my last reserves.

At that time Helen refused to let me in, saying that my father had forbidden me any access to the house. I was too busted to challenge the rejection. I had rather expected it, and I trudged off into the bitterly cold winter afternoon, a huge duffel bag over my shoulder. It would have been easiest, I remember thinking, to find a secluded place and just lie down, go to sleep and freeze to death. In the preceding weeks I had been marooned in a blizzard with minus forty degree temperatures while hitchhiking through northern Ontario. I was weary of this kind of life on the edge. I just wanted to be warm for a while. During my school years, there had been winter nights when I had had nowhere to go and I had taken the train or bus into Toronto. In the dead of winter, bums fought over places on the vents from the subway system. They would huddle over them and sleep there, the warm air sustaining them from the bitter cold in the middle of the broad sidewalks, oblivious to pedestrians passing all around. I would loiter for hours in the Union train station or spend whole nights riding on the subways. I had always survived, but my spirit had never been as low as it was that bitter January afternoon. I was worn out, too shattered to care any longer. I dug into my last resource, a final remaining pocketful of change, and took the chance of finding some long lost cousins who lived in Mississauga, a suburb of Toronto. There was just enough change for a one way fare without even one more dime for a payphone. It was my last shot. I stepped off the commuter train at the station closest to their home and plodded through the ankle-deep grey slush. It never froze because of all the road salt. The briny ice mixture soon seeped into my boots, until my feet were wet and numb with cold. I remember that long walk along the suburban winter streets, the damp wind blowing off the lake with an acid bite. There had been a smell of snow in the air and I had fought the urge to fall down among the frozen garbage and dog shit lying in the dirty snow and go to sleep. I tramped along, one painful, weary step after another until finally I arrived at my destination.

Mercifully my cousins were home. I collapsed through their front doorway. Both women lived in the same house with their husbands and children so one more mouth to feed was of no great consequence to them. These were the same cousins who had cared for me at times when I was a small child and they were well aware of what I had endured at my parent's hands. Horrified at my plight, they brought me into their home. Despite their own limited resources, they nurtured me and gave me a bed. I stayed in their basement throughout the winter. Unable to find steady work, I subsisted shamefully on the charity of these two families. Finally borrowing a little money in the spring, I returned to British Columbia and the promise of a job that had crumbled as soon as I arrived. In retrospect, that winter had been the lowest point in my life. If there had been no-one home that night in Mississauga, I would surely have died, my body just another nameless, frozen corpse found under a bridge, a cadaver perhaps for a medical university.

Now this was the first time that I had returned to the old house since that winter afternoon, nearly thirty years ago. I knew that I would not be standing there if my father still lived here. The house was painted garishly and was visibly crumbling. The yard was a terrible mess and there was a sense of sadness to it all, like an abandoned amusement park. When I had lived at home, on the tiny porch at the top of the steps to the backdoor, my parents had kept a large metal garbage can, which took up most of the porch but was handy to the kitchen. To my relief I noticed that it was no longer there and wondered why I had intuitively focused on the can. Most of my memories centre on some insignificant object, and the garbage can was no exception. One day, while putting some trash in the can, I found several men's magazines mysteriously stashed in the bottom. I was a twelve year old with a natural, intense curiosity with regard to anything about sex. The magazines were soon re-stowed under my mattress and wildly stimulated my adolescent libido. They were a huge graduation from the women's lingerie section in the Sears and Eaton's catalogues.

Weeks later, in an uncharacteristic burst of domestic ambition, mother had done some cleaning in my room and discovered my secret. Sex was the ultimate taboo to her and anything to do with it was instantly labelled as disgusting and filthy. In a rage she confronted me with the magazines and I tried to explain where I'd found them. 'That father of yours is a pervert and a sex maniac and now you're trying to be just like him. Show me what's so interesting in those evil books!' She made me open one and leaf through it page by page until I finally arrived at a photograph of a seductively and explicitly posed naked nymph. 'Female Breasts', she screamed, 'The only tits that should interest you are these!' She tore open her blouse, exposing her own breasts hanging like two small, shrivelled old pears. The sight disgusted and horrified me. 'These are what kept you alive when you were a baby,' she raged on. 'Didn't I feed you enough, do you still need to suck them?' She advanced toward me her blouse held high. The image of those moments is indelibly etched in my memory. How I had wanted to hit her. But how do you strike a woman, especially your mother, when she is making such a vulgar and pathetic display?

When it was clear that she had successfully humiliated me with her ridiculous behaviour and her rage began to turn to embarrassment, she tried to debase me further. 'Look at these sheets,' she bellowed, 'They're stained as badly as a newlyweds! This is absolute filth, get on your knees and beg God to forgive you for this disgusting animal behaviour!' I refused - terrified, humiliated, and furious. My mother was venturing into new territory and I did not know how to deal her. Her incredible outburst would rage on for hours. I felt totally defeated, realizing that there were few aspects of my life where I could avoid my parents' intrusions. They had no respect for me as a person, let alone their son. They seemed to regard me as a chattel, their possession to be abused as they chose. 'Just wait until your father gets home. We'll get to the bottom of this!' Of course he denied any knowledge of the magazines and accused me of lying about how I had come by them. I was totally devastated, first by mother's perverse rage, and now that my father as usual would not admit his part in the scenario. I felt set up, hung out to dry, yet again a pawn in their endless war with each other.

As a result of that incident my mother decided that it was 'high time that I learned the facts of life'. Throughout the following weeks she set about the most incredibly convoluted, confusingly contorted explanation about the origins of life. I stoically endured her stumbling efforts that were mixed with massive doses of scripture and prayer. I was repeatedly quoted the biblical admonition about, 'spilling my seed on the ground'. The message she offered ultimately suggested that sex was the lowest debasement of human existence. Clearly, children were the carnal product of a base and contemptible act. At that age, despite my sheltered upbringing, I was already far better informed about sex than my mother apparently was, and I marvelled at her weird and perverse aversion to a basic human function. My father also had a strange approach to human biology, and I wondered at my parents' need to be so perverse, all the while trying to hide their abstract notions under the thin guise of piety and a Christian sense of decency.

Ironically, within two years, only a short time after my mother had left my father, I would be seduced by a friend's mother, a very attractive, affluent, bored lady who was leading a life of quite desperation. Oakville was the most affluent community in Canada at that time. There was a constant undercurrent of decadence and hedonistic indulgence, which lay beneath a thin crust of conservative facade and elegant opulence. While compassionate to my plight, she also capitalized on my vulnerability and used me for her own amusement. Not that I minded. Unconsciously I was rebelling against the pious facade which had smothered me for so long. At the time I felt grown up and needed, perhaps even loved. Sadly it was but another way that I was manipulated and victimized by someone criminally irresponsible for my welfare and my desperately low self-esteem.

Perhaps she did truly care, and simply had a unique way of demonstrating her concern. Certainly she plied me with an extraordinary private education, generous amounts of cash and clothing. She offered me the assurance that she would help me whenever I needed it, although she made it clear that my role was to serve when and as it suited her. I knew that I had to be incredibly discreet but doubted anyone would believe the truth if it were discovered. I tried to maintain an apparently normal friendship with her son, but he distanced himself; of course he had to have some notion of what was occurring. In later years I learned that I was not the only boy she had used in the same way. I understood then that I was entirely expendable to this woman, a mere toy among her distractions, especially when she began to introduce me to her friends, informing me that she had recommended my services to them. It forced me further into the maze of a double life. That I was incredibly confused is a mild understatement. How I avoided becoming a derelict in those years of my youth is both a mystery and a miracle.

I felt that, to have any friends and to continue being a self-sufficient high school student, I had to appear as much as possible to be a typical, normal teenager. I was not sure of what normal was. Despite taking secret pride in my carnal industry, I felt incredibly insecure and self-conscious among my peers. Most teenage boys were obsessed with sex and their ignorance about it. I carefully pretended to possess a similar naiveté. I spent my entire high school years hiding my secret life and wrestling with the interminable conflicts that it brought. I was already confused and completely disoriented simply by being a teenager. My family situation and the programming I received as a child kept me on the eternally edge of shame and despair. The implications of being essentially a child prostitute led me into another dimension, one that produced an inextricable demoralization and perplexity about what was real, what was fantasy, what was acceptable, and what was not. In addition to my clandestine activities, I also held a part-time job to support myself well enough to be able to attend school. Those years as a teenager were a grind, but some inner spark kept me determined not to succumb to failure and mediocrity. In the end, I graduated with a scholarship. Unfortunately I had been denied the opportunity of enjoying my teenage years.

As I look back now from adulthood I do not regret my experiences, knowing that they have been both positive and negative. I will always suspect women's motives, even after I established lasting relationships. I have regarded sex as a sort of duty instead of a mutual expression of affection. I know with certainty, despite all the mystique, that women need and enjoy the animal pleasure of copulation as much as men. At the time I believed mine was a unique situation. Only later would I understand that my experience was not at all uncommon. In fact, I am incredibly fortunate about how my life has turned out, yes, even as miserable as I have unwittingly made it. Many young people who fall into the entanglements of the sex trade have a sadly short and hopeless life. There are many horrific tragedies that continue to occur around the simple facts of human biology. I realize that, despite the perverse sexual attitudes of my parents, what I had experienced was neither immoral nor unwholesome. I am grateful for my candid attitude about sex versus the stigmas that so many others hold. I also muse that perhaps at that time I had found a necessary substitute for maternal love. However, I cannot condone any self gratification that humans seem determined to impose on the vulnerable and the innocent.

Once inside the old house, I was appalled at how tiny the place was, at how incredibly tacky and run down it seemed. While Helen prepared dinner I looked around. I went into the basement, with its five foot head room under the massive rough-cut floor beams. To stand erect, you had to carefully raise your head between the beams. The root cellar, with its familiar smell exactly the same as it was thirty years earlier, stood in one corner. I was vaguely surprised that there was no longer any preserved fruit or produce on its shelves. The same damned old ringer-washer machine sat in another corner. It may have been replaced by a newer one but still seemed to menace me from where it lurked in the corner. I remembered getting my arm drawn between the rollers some times while I did the laundry, then packing the heavy wet clothes up the steep stairs and hanging them from the clothes line on the porch by the backdoor. Laundry frozen stiff in the winter, wet in the summer rain, once a week, wash-day

Monday, every damned Monday after school, do the laundry and make supper, a horrible Macaroni and tomato sauce with hamburger meal. Come to think of it, that was part of the misery of my childhood, the predictable same meal for each night of the week. The same smothered feeling I had known as a boy in this same cellar once again enveloped me with its frustration and sadness.

In the opposite corner of the basement stood a rough workbench my father had built - it remained the same as I remembered. I had sat at it for hours, building plastic model airplanes, listening to the radio station CHUM in Toronto play the hits of the day. The music was from a world where I did not live but longed to be. I blinked back more bitter tears and could see myself sitting there and heard the songs again. Last Kiss, Help, I Wanna Hold your Hand, Henry the Eighth I Am, Love Potion Number Nine, Downtown... I could spend a long time reminiscing and not begin to remember all of the tunes.

On ascending from the cellar, a trap door closed over the stairs and a double-hinged ladder could then be pulled down on top of the trap door. This provided access to the attic, which is where I went now. I was shocked to notice that I could see through several cracks in the lath and plaster of the ceiling and realized again that the house should be condemned. It had been slightly renovated from a derelict shell when my father had first rented it thirty-five years before and was long overdue to be razed. The attic still had the same musty smell, the same shredded paper insulation, the open joists to step on with the risk of slipping and falling through the ceiling, the same little windows that looked out at either end of the house. I had been away for over thirty years, travelled and lived around the planet and not one speck of dust seemed out of place from when I had last stood here.

Dinner was a success. The meal was simple fare,

poorly cooked, but I knew it was Helen's best effort and I ate happily, immersed in conversation with her and Susan about funny events and anecdotes from the past. Helen finally mentioned the last time that I had been to this house and how she had turned me away. She tried to apologize and I stopped her, saying there was nothing to explain, that I now understood how my father had managed to manipulate nearly everyone. He had even managed to keep my brother and me apart for nearly twenty years. I was touched that she remembered that particular day and had felt guilty about it through the years. It all seemed so long ago, the bleakness and bitterness of my surreal existence then, now balanced against the surreal events of the moment. Dinner over, pleasantries and assurances all in place, I took my leave of the old house one final time. I arranged to leave the vehicle in the driveway when I had finished with it. I returned to my father's apartment.

The next morning I rose after another rum-induced rest. Bereft of sound sleep, I felt groggy and exhausted. The day lay ahead. It was to be the last time that I would ever be with my father. I resolved that, before going home, I would take an extra day to drive through some of my old haunts in the surrounding countryside, looking for happy memories, trying to find some of the places that I had not seen in so very long. After breakfast, I waited impatiently for a flower shop to open and bought the most fragrant roses available. In the hospital elevator I suddenly noticed my beating heart, my sweaty hands, and was acutely aware of the smallest nondescript details: scratches and handprints on the railing of the elevator, the sound of a nurse's soft-soled shoes in the hallway, various other tiny noises. There was a metallic taste in my mouth. Time and distance passed in lurches and I wanted to run away from this dreadful moment. I stopped to compose myself, assuring myself that this was the hardest part of all, but it would soon be over and then my life would be on its way back to becoming normal. 'Courage, man, courage, just remember how tired you are, be careful not to overreact.'

Stepping into his room, I watched the old man snoring slightly in his sleep, and wondered how many times I had watched him sleeping. It was something he had always been able to do, to fall asleep anywhere at any time, often napping in the most improbable places. He seemed to look so peaceful and I was well aware that I would never see my father alive again. 'Not long till the big nap now, you old fart,' I though to myself. My eyes welled with tears. I laid the large bouquet of roses gently on my father's chest and went to see the nurses to thank them for their patience and care with my father. I knew their task was horrific and that it was a job I could never begin to do. When I finished this visit I suspected I would be leaving abruptly and wanted to express my gratitude while I was still reasonably composed.

When I returned to the bedside, the old man was waking up. I bid him a cheery good morning, explaining about the roses, and said I hoped that he liked them, knowing that roses were the ultimate pleasure for my father. 'Their smell woke me up,' he said, 'Thought I was dead and on me way to heaven.' He seemed disappointed to still be alive. I noticed how the old man's broad English Midland's accent had thickened and it was pleasing to hear its course lyrical rhythm. 'Well, Dad, I've come to say good-bye today. We both knew this was coming. I have to go home to my family and my life.' 'Yes, my boy, I know you do. There's nothing else you can do here.'

I continued, a little lost for words, 'I wish there was something else I could do, but everything is in order... everything is looked after. All the arrangements are complete with Rudy... when the time comes.... I'll make sure your ashes go on roses in a nice place.... in Nanaimo. That way at least you'll finally be staying as close as possible to us in B.C. and.....' Suddenly I found myself cradling the old man's head in my arms, weeping and shuddering uncontrollably. My father misunderstood the emotion, not knowing that I wept for all the wasted years, all that would never be, all the pain and mediocrity. 'It's all right, son, I know how you feel. Don't worry. I'm ready to meet my maker. Thank you for looking after everything. I didn't expect it.... not after all these years. I've not been much of a father I know, I've had mental problems and I got it all wrong.' 'It's all right, I know you did the best you could,' I muttered while thinking, 'No, you still don't have a clue how I feel, you old prick!' There was something that made me want to snap the old man's neck while I held him, still a need for vindication and revenge, justice, a wilful end to all the years of evil. It frightened me and I had to leave. 'Well, Dad, I know you're in good hands here and they'll do their best to keep you comfortable. I have to say good bye now. God be with you.'

I turned and left, looking back one last time, my father cradling the roses, savouring their smell, the blank blissful, blind look back on his face. 'Fuck! He doesn't even know what fucking planet he's on'. I slammed out through the double doors at the end of the hall, torrents of tears gushing uncontrollably down my face. I found an unoccupied room that looked out on the spring morning in all its golden glory and stood at the window, letting the pent-up frustration and fatigue wash to the surface and then away. Five minutes later I was able to compose myself thinking, 'Right then, you silly bastard, you've done your best, now fuck the rest, there's nothing more you can do here. Let's get on with it.' I strode to the elevator and pushed the button, hoping that it would arrive unoccupied. It wasn't. I smiled bravely at an old lady in a wheelchair, and a beautiful younger woman, probably her daughter, who accompanied her. She smiled back. 'Well then, life goes on,' I thought as I strode out in the sunshine.

The morning seemed to progress like a prolonged scene from a surreal 'Art Nouveau' movie. Time passed in a dreamy way. It seemed to take hours for things to happen. The light was low and soft as I drove along the main street of my old home town, quite possibly for the last time ever. The car radio began to play a plaintive, poignant melody with trumpets and strings that tore at my soul. My eyes blurred with tears once again. I had to pull to the side of the street, unable to drive. 'The scene fades now,' I thought, 'The credits roll to a background of syrupy music and the movie ends after the good-bye scene with the dying father.' I tried to shrug the feeling off and drive away but a few blocks later, the dying notes of the music still grasped me. I turned back into town and drove to the radio station to learn the name of the tune. It turned out to be 'Charmaine' by Montavani. 'Just great,' I thought, 'The old man isn't even dead yet and here I am getting turned on by the same old fart tunes that he'd go for.'

A wave of exhaustion washed over me as I drove back to the apartment, wondering what to do next, yet too tired to really care or think about what I was doing. I collapsed on the couch, feeling grateful that things were beginning to wind down. I was incredulous about what all had transpired in five days, and was amazed to realize that a week earlier I had still been at work aboard a tugboat at sea off the west coast. Finally, I fell asleep.

Late in the afternoon I was awakened by a loud, authoritative knock at the door. I rose up groggy and disoriented, and stumbled toward the door while trying to dress. Again someone pounded insistently on the door and I bent to the peep hole. Standing in the hall was Greg, the apartment manager. He was dwarfed by three huge black men. They all looked alike: at least six and a half feet tall, broad-shouldered, very dark, each with a huge head of frizzy hair and all wearing a black trench coat with the collar drawn up. 'Oh fuck,' I thought, 'What now? The Russian dwarf and the three ugly black giants?' I considered not answering the door but then realized that they would have a key for the door and that they were there about rent money. 'Will this fucking nightmare ever fucking end,' I mused as I prepared myself to open the door, realizing that the best hope of defence was a very aggressive offence. I swung the door open abruptly, 'Yes?'

One of the blacks stepped forward, pushing past Greg who stood there with a helpless, apologetic look on his face. 'Heh, mon, my name is Rufé, how are you today?' 'Actually not very good,' I replied as flatly as possible. 'What can I do for you?' 'Well, mon, we understan' dat you are leavin' dis place wit no notice. We need two monts rent!'

'Look man,' I replied, my voice rising, 'I don't owe you fuck all. Why don't you find out who you are talking to before you start making demands from a total stranger. This is my father's apartment. He's in the hospital dying. If you want two months rent, go try winding him up and see how you make out..... man!'

'Look, we represent de management, we jus tryin' to do our job, mon. Can we come in an talk about dis?' I had visions of being flung off the balcony or at least going home with a broken leg and was resolved that I would go down fighting. 'There's nothing to talk about. I've cleaned up this filthy, fucking ghetto your management has the balls to charge an old man six hundred and fifty dollars a month for. I should be charging you money. If it weren't for Greg and me, you'd have this apartment sitting here with the walls smeared with shit and a rotting body inside, so tell your management that things are turning out pretty good for them. Now I'm going to pack my bags and go back home to British Columbia where I live and I'll leave the rest up to you. So piss off out of my face and leave me alone. I've got enough problems without your bullshit. Have a good day!' 'You mean, you don' live aroun' here mon?' 'Look, I've told you, this is my father's apartment. You'll get nothing out of me. Furthermore, if it takes three of you pussies to come around to try and harass old men like this, you're going to get the 911 treatment right now!' I slammed the door and slid the deadbolt home.

I was shaking, from both my rage and terror. 'I can't take any more of this crap,' I thought, 'I've got to get away from here. That was too ugly for me.' Five minutes later I cautiously looked through the peephole and there was no one in the hall. I resolved that by morning I would be gone.

Chapter 4

CRUISING

I was awake at first light the next morning. I had slept reasonably well, but still felt worn and wrung out. I showered and packed my bags, wrote a short note for Greg to explain that I was gone and to thank him for the help that he had provided. 'No way I'm waiting around for the three nightmares to come back,' I thought. 'Let's blow this Popsicle stand.' In another ten minutes I was driving down Kerr Street. It was seven o'clock in the morning.

I wondered how many miles I had walked up and down this street as a boy. I passed the grocery store where I had worked as a stock-boy, the same store where I used to wait in the snow and rain to pick up my newspapers for delivery. There was the street where I had boarded when I was fourteen years old. A huge old Slavic woman had charged me ten dollars a week for bed and breakfast, wondering gruffly in her broken English why such a young boy was living on his own. Many of the shops and businesses were still in the same location as when I had lived here and I wondered what it must be like to have a life that never changed.

My life had been nothing but change, always moving on, driven, seeking a better opportunity, running from what appeared to be imminent crisis but only creating a worse one because of my lack of stability. I realized how good life might have been if only I had clung to some of the opportunities that I had passed by. Then I considered how rich my life had become with more experiences than three average lifetimes could hold, and I suddenly saw my regrets and failures as achievements. At least I had dreamt of rising above the mediocrity that I saw all around me and which I abhorred. The thought of a life like that makes me shudder with dread. I know that, because I have never stayed with anything for long, I have risked a fate perhaps worse than mediocrity, but at least I have tried to follow my heart. I wondered again about my old classmates, where they were, what they now did, what they looked like, and I considered that by now, at least a few must be dead. I also knew that many had never really lived nor ever would.

At the bottom of the street I turned onto the old Lakeshore Highway and drove west until finally I came to Bronte. When I had last been here it was a miserable little village at the mouth of the Twelve Mile Creek. As a boy I had bicycled to the creek mouth and shot at carp in the marshes with a bow. There had been a few shops and some blocks of ramshackle houses, a quick stop on the road between Hamilton and Oakville. Now it was a pretty little town, filled with trendy shops and boutiques, with 'something for every kind of yuppie'. The once boggy harbour mouth had been excavated and was now the site of a large modern marina jammed with expensive yachts. Being an avid sailor who spends as much time as possible cruising the coastal waters of British Columbia, I marvelled at the investments people made in yachts. There are few places to go on Lake Ontario, no anchorages and a boating season that ends when the lake and its harbours freeze solid for several months each winter.

I stopped for a quick breakfast and then drove north to a place known as Palermo Corners. This marked an intersection with an east-west highway known as the King's Highway, the Dundas Highway or simply highway five. Running north and south was a main road between Bronte and Milton, highway twenty-five. I turned east now, driving toward another place that was a significant memory from my past, doubting that I would recognize anything. Suddenly I was on the bridge crossing the Sixteen Mile Creek. I recognized where I was, only a mile from the site of the Lingren Farm where my father had worked as a hired hand when I was just three years old. It was hard to remember all the places we had lived and to piece together our history. My mother had once told me that we had changed jobs and homes thirteen times before moving to town when I was about five years old.

Past the bridge, on the east bank of the creek, stood an old red brick church. I had gone to my first wedding there and hated all weddings ever since, including my own. While preparing for that first one, mother had slammed the car door on my small fingers, almost severing one and I had to be rushed to the hospital for repairs. I could still remember my screaming terror as the doctor sutured my fingers, and the huge bandage on my throbbing hand while I sat in the hot, stuffy church at the wedding ceremony later that afternoon.

A little further along the road I noticed a huge realty sign beside the highway. Then I saw the barn. Incredible! This was the place! The small house where we'd lived was gone. There was just a slight concavity in the corner of the field by the lane where it had stood, but I recognized the lane, its over-hanging trees, the Lingren's old house and behind that, the barn. Beyond the barn had been rambling fields, bordered by huge elm and ash trees, with thickets of spruce and pine. At the back of one field, a huge woodland of twenty or more acres had once stood; it had seemed like an endless forest to me then. I went there with my parents once to cut a Christmas tree. Snow covered everything, the sun sparkled through the trees and flakes of frost glistened as they drifted down on the crisp air. My father had cleared the snow from on top of the ice covering a small clear stream that ran in the woods, and I had seen small black minnows swimming under the ice. Sometimes I still dream about those little fish.

Later, my mother had been in hospital with appendicitis and two cousins came to look after me, the same ones whose charity I would later seek. Both girls were then in their early teens and were concerned about me wandering off into the woods, a favourite place for me. They incessantly warned me about the 'Boogie Man' and finally took me one dusky evening to the gate across the path into the woods. They had hung a straw-stuffed effigy in old work cloths in the trees where it dangled by its neck. It swayed gently from a limb as the rising evening wind murmured through the trees. The image is indelible, but I cannot recall if it had the desired effect of frightening me. Now the woodlot was no longer there. It had been turned into a golf course. The fields were now a sprawling subdivision with curving rows of identical box-like houses - a depressing, hopeless sight.

I parked my father's vehicle in the same place that our old Ford had once sat and stood there looking around. I remembered so much, happy memories as well as more of the sordid ones. I had been given a kitten named Sparky; a photo had been taken of myself and the kitten crouching inside a huge tin lard pail that I used to store my toys. There had apparently been a puppy before, but for some reason it had not been around long and nor could I remember what happened to the kitten.

Years later, while re-reading this book, the memory of what had happened to the puppy came to me. I awoke from a dreamless sleep in the middle of the night in my bunk at sea, and suddenly relived the horror, nearly fifty years later. Thunk, thunk, thunk! I could again vividly hear the dull slam and ring of the shovel as dad smashed the writhing pup. Perhaps it had chewed one of his bootlaces, one excuse would have been as good as another. I was playing in the backyard with the young dog at the time, giggling in delight as it licked me and wriggled happily in my arms, my very best, my only friend, the perfect bond, a young boy and his first dog, a new puppy. *In a typical surge of vindictive rage dad had seized the yelping pup in one hand and me in another. Beside the barn he killed my dog before my eyes then thrust the shovel at me to bury it in the manure pile. I could not do it and was scorned for my weakness. The pup's little pink tongue now hung flaccid and speckled in dirt. Only minutes earlier it had licked me face with undiluted love. The skull was a bloodied pulp, one eyeball distended from its socket, and staring seeping blood steamed in the cool of the evening. A hole was finally dug. The still warm body of my pup, now limp, mashed and bloodied carrion, was flung contemptuously into the pit and covered with reeking cow shit. I barely remember the choking horror of that evening and the days that followed - the terrible sense of loss, my shock of malicious violence toward something so purely innocent, so undeserving of malice for any reason. However, as a man in his mid-fifties, I know the effect of that trauma is insidiously subtle and eternal. Only I can know what other dark memories are locked deep within my psyche.*

The pup was the lucky one I think. Perhaps it would have been merciful of my father if he had killed me then as well. The entire event, which must have occurred within a matter of minutes, had been locked deep within the back my memory for all of my life. Thankfully I cannot remember what happened to the kitten. I believe I begin to understand another corner of my own insecurities. Nothing lasts, especially if it has to do with love and security. That night, as usual, I can be confident that I was made to somehow feel responsible for the carnage and loss. I can only surmise that within the litany of demented horrors that so often clouded my childhood this was a central event toward both my tremendous insecurity and residual anger. There have been shameful times in my life when my rage has led me to irresponsible and unforgivable destructiveness, both physical and psychological, just as I had been taught. Sadly those tempests have been directed at people who were the least deserving, and in fact were often those who dared to love me despite my pathetic flaws. I will live eternally with a sense of loss and guilt for the pain I have caused. I have alienated people whom I will dearly miss for the rest of my days. I pray to all of the gods of the universe that those whom I so abused have been able to heal from their ordeals at my hand and have been able to find a full and happy life.

I have outgrown those violent urges, yet knowing that I am my father's son is a frightening and heavy, permanent burden. Is it any single event or an accumulation of ongoing trauma that shape a child's character? The answer is twice yes, but no excuse is acceptable whether or not any adult realizes their own aberrant tendencies. Acknowledging a problem is a first step, fully accepting responsibility is the next. People can change, but they must want to.

The highway by the old farm was long and straight; cars rushed past the house night and day. There were accidents. Occasionally someone would come to the door in the middle of the night, their face often bloody. There had been a car wreck and it was necessary to phone for help. A fishmonger, incongruously called Mr. Pike, used to come by once a week in a truck filled with fresh fish on ice. Our family had lived here during the vicious onslaught of Hurricane Hazel. I recalled sitting inside the window watching the low, dark, scudding clouds and the driving rain. Water rose steadily over the highway and the fields. Vehicles sloshed slowly along the highway and the milk truck had become stuck in the ditch while trying to find the turn into the farm. It had taken several days for life to return to normal after the storm.

Waves of disconnected memories washed over me as I stood there. I realized with amazement that I had not even been three years old at the time. For some reason I suddenly remembered a weekly publication called the 'Family Herald', a magazine directed at families living on farms. I also recalled hours happily spent looking and fantasizing through both the Sears and Eaton's catalogues; at that age I was intrigued with the toy section and the firearms. Again I heard the radio playing and the voice announcing: 'The six o'clock CBC evening news as read by Walter Bowls.'

My father would plod up the lane from the barn for supper. Too tired to take off his coveralls, he would sit at the table with his feet on a mat, frozen mud and manure melting off his gumboots while he sat there. On several occasions he fell asleep at the table, sometimes ending up with his face in his plate. Then he would go back to the barn to work on into the night, tending a sow delivering piglets, cleaning up the dairy and the stalls; there was often something to keep him there working alone into the night. In the morning he would rise long before dawn and begin the morning milking, which was still done by hand then. This routine went on seven days a week. That was the way life was on a dairy farm, the pay a pittance, the work mostly manual labour. The smell of cow shit pervaded everything, even in church on Sunday morning with everyone freshly bathed and wearing their best clothes.

This was the home where I had begun doing chores at a tender age. There were no other children for miles around with whom to play, and my parents both seemed to be eternally engaged in some sort of activity. I naturally assumed a habitual work ethic which both parents used to their advantage. I had begun cooking at that age, dragging a stool to stand up at the stove, stirring pots of porridge and soup. That I had not been scalded or badly burned is amazing.

Although the family lived on dairy farms, for some reason we consumed margarine and powdered, skimmed milk. The margarine came in soft plastic bags with a tiny bead of food colouring in one side of the bag. It was pure white, like lard, and if a buttery colour was desired, one broke the bead of dye and worked it into the margarine. That was one of my jobs, squeezing the bag of margarine around and around until my small hands ached, but it fascinated me to watch the bead become a swirl of red colour that eventually dissolved into an even yellow shade. I also mixed the powdered milk, which was often lumpy and thin. The taste always disgusted me but it was what the family drank and drizzled over our bowls of lumpy tasteless porridge each morning.

It was odd that, although the family was surrounded by an abundance of good, fresh food, we often ate poorly, consuming barely palatable fare, which would often be heaped on my plate. I would be forced to eat everything served to me. If I could not finish my food, I would often have to gulp it down cold at the next meal. This was supposed to teach me to appreciate the privilege of having something to eat. I would always hear my father's weary line about 'waste not, want not'. There were endless accounts of eating war rations in England and mother had her yarns of tough times, 'back on the homestead in the dirty thirties'. She incessantly preserved fruit and vegetables, baked bread, and kept a garden, but it seemed the family usually ate pathetically, as if it were a virtue to endure paltry, tasteless sustenance, or evil to enjoy well-cooked, tasty meals.

When there were no more kitchen duties, there were still household chores, or firewood and ashes to struggle with. When everything indoors was accomplished, there was always the damned garden to be weeded and dug, rocks to be moved and vegetables to harvest. It was a hollow existence for a young child, essentially still an infant, but it seemed that suffering was a deliberate way of life and misery was something to embrace above all other human sensations. I now mused about how this confused indoctrination deeply and permanently deformed my personality and my understanding of how the world around me worked. I have gone through my entire life, punishing and denying myself fulfilment and a sense of well-being that I nevertheless eternally ache for. Despite my best efforts, what I know in my head cannot find a place in my heart.

When all the work for the moment was finally done, I was left to amuse myself alone. Like a common farm animal, when I could no longer be exploited, I was turned loose and forgotten until needed again. I invented friends and amusements to pass my free time and delighted in simply observing nature, be it insect life in the weeds or clouds in the sky. I learned to observe and mentally record minute details. As an adult I often curse myself for the deep memory of most of my childhood. I often wish I could obliterate it. However, perhaps because they were so rare, I cherish memories of any happy events and of the times when my parents did share a good experience with me.

As my mind strayed to the things that I had been able to call my own as a child, I realized that most of my toys had been given to me by family friends and relatives. Prized possessions included a green plastic tumbler with the picture a calf on it, something my father had brought from the barn. There was also a steel radiator cap, probably from an ancient Pontiac because it was cast in the shape of an Indian chief's head. The bottom was threaded where it screwed onto the car's radiator. Heavy, cracked, the chrome pitted and peeling, it was a precious object and served for many years as a paper weight and door-stop. It was now long lost. What I would give now to hold it my hand again, that piece of discarded scrap metal. A child's most precious treasures are usually nondescript. As an adult, I still value most highly things that most others consider only junk.

Morning doves sat on the wires overhead softly cooing their soothing song as they had when I was a child. Looking across the fields I remembered my view of this same place through infant eyes and I longed for that sense of wonder again. What magic, seeing something for the first time. It seemed there was always also a dark memory that loomed up to cast a shadow on a happy one. I recalled another incident involving that same old Ford car. I lay in the back seat while my father drove as fast as he dared, blasting the horn and cursing with impatience. My mother had discarded some pills in the garbage. I had found them and eaten the entire contents of the bottle. I awakened in the emergency room at the hospital, gagging on a plastic tube that had been inserted down my throat to pump my stomach. A doctor stood there in his white coat, a round, doughnut-shaped mirror on a headband over his forehead, stethoscope around his neck. He smiled broadly and informed me about what a lucky boy I was. 'A few minutes later and it would have been too late.' There followed a horrible row between my father and mother on the drive home. I was feeling quite ill, and endured the shouting in the front seat about the careless disposal of my mother's 'nerve pills'. Both parents were more interested in having something new to fight about than the simple, thankful joy that their only child was still alive.

That brought another darker memory about this same rolling farmland. I recalled being carried in my mother's arms, gripped fiercely as she ran sobbing through the fields in the dark. She had run on and on until we became entangled in a loose barbed wire fence where we were snared like panic-stricken animals. Blood, sharp pain, my mother's hysterical sobbing were eventually followed by the frightening beams of flashlights approaching eerily through the mist settling across the fields. A small search party finally found us. What had triggered the incident was lost to me but I could still recall my terror of my mother and the dread of the mystery that had driven her to flight.

In balance, the first Christmas that I can ever recall was here. I had been absolutely delighted to wake to the sight of the fields covered in an unbroken blanket of deep, fresh snow that had fallen overnight. In the morning light the undulating countryside sparkled and glowed in untracked, pristine purity. It was shortly before Christmas. Everything seemed magical and every waking minute had a sweet intensity. My mother's birthday was not until the end of the first week in December and it was only after that when radio stations began playing carols and ads for Christmas shopping. Mother busied herself with extra baking through the day and secret projects that she worked at until late at night. When Christmas Eve arrived, I was excited as only a young child could be. A Christmas tree now stood in the small living room, laden with decorations and a few coloured lights. I was just old enough to comprehend the myth of Santa Claus and sat in my small crib in my darkened room too agitated for sleep, waiting for something, anything to happen. When my father opened the bedroom door to check on me, I wet the bed, thinking it was Santa arriving. I seldom wet the bed because of the spanking I knew was forthcoming, but it was Christmas and for once I was dealt with compassionately. 'What a Christmas memory,' I considered, *'Not* getting a spanking'.

In the soft, bright, first light of Christmas morning, I had ventured into the living room, morning-cold yet, the woodstove unlit, my parents still asleep. Under the tree sat a doll. I can still hear my own whoop of joy and how I had instantly named the doll Peter. Mother had made it, a life-sized, stuffed rag doll dressed in some of my own clothing that I had outgrown. Peter wore coveralls, a plaid shirt, a wool toque and a small pair of leather boots. There was a permanent smile embroidered on his cotton face. I cannot remember anything else about that Christmas. I was an only child, living with my parents miles from other children, and Peter was a tangible companion who accompanied me everywhere. Years later, at the age of twelve or thirteen, the doll had been long relegated to the back of the closet, tattered and filthy. Yet when my mother threw the doll in the garbage, I was furious with her. I still resent that loss. In retrospect, the doll represented a tangible effort of my mother to give something enduring of herself, something that she would have increasing difficulty doing as the years went by. I was thankful for the lasting memory of that precious gift, her labour of love.

I looked at the slight indentation in the ground where that old house had once stood, brief vignettes of memory rolling by in my mind like some flickering old home-movie. Fragmented as they were, inaccurate as they might be, bleak as they often were, it was still a connection to my past, my 'roots' as people call them, and I wondered why memories, even bad ones, are of such value to humans. I realized how insignificant this place would be to anyone else and yet this precise location had once been the centre of my universe, small as it may have been. Here was the yard where I had played, there the garden, there would have been the wood lot, there still stood the barn.

The barn! I walked toward it down the lane as if in a dream. I vaguely remembered that I had occasionally accompanied my father there, and had even been left to play alone in the loft while Dad worked in the stables below. That was more than forty years ago. I approached the now crumbling building with a strange sense of trepidation and fascination, like a child working up the courage to enter a supposed haunted house.

I walked past the foundations of the barn built from stones gathered as the fields were cleared. The hand-hewn timbers were beginning to rot in places and I was amazed to realize how old the building might be. I stepped inside, incredulous that this old dairy barn still held the same smell after all the years. Manure, dust, spilled milk, hay, it was not the fresh acrid smell of a working barn, it was mellow and mature, like a fine wine, this aroma of the old dairy barn and oh, how smell can stimulate memory!

I looked at the once white-washed timbers of the milking stalls, the curving, rusted overhead track that carried a manure trolley out through a hole in the wall, the steel rings on the stanchions, the smooth-rubbed staves of the feed cribs, and once again I was a toddler, looking up at my father and other workers as they bent to their labours. I could hear the lowing of the cows, punctuated with an occasional bellow. The splash of body-warm milk hitting an empty milk bucket, my father's head resting against the flank of a cow as his thick fingers rhythmically massaged the milk out of the cow's teats. I could see the flicking, manure-sloppy tail of the cows and the barn cats that would come, meowing as they begged for a squirt of milk into their mouths. Often the cows lifted their tails and a deluge of steaming shit would splatter into the gutter at the back of the stalls. Slowly I walked through the barn and even though it was now stacked with someone's stored building supplies, my memories of this place expanded in rapid succession. I marvelled, how after such a long time, they were still so vivid. I could still feel the dark and bitter winter chill outside and the musky animal warmth inside the barn. There is a sense of security and well-being like nothing else in a barn full of farm animals. Even though the creatures were long-gone and the barn would obviously soon be demolished, I felt that I had found a piece of home that I wanted to retain.

There was the stall where two workhorses were kept. I could still see the old Clydesdale gnawing the top board of the enclosure. The thick, soft, fuzzy lips were drawn back from the huge, pink gums and massive yellow teeth as they worked at the heavy plank. That gnawed board was still there, exactly the same! In the corner was where the pigs were kept. I could see the huge sow laying on her side, a dozen tiny, pink piglets eagerly pushing at each other, feverishly suckling at the double row of nipples along her belly. I could hear the desperate scream of the baby boars as they were being castrated. I could still see my father's bloodied hands and his knife as he reached for yet another piglet.

Here was the hay chute from the loft above and the steep set of stairs that had been such a challenge to me as a toddler the last time that I had stood in this same spot! There were so many steep challenges in life. All the connecting events, moments, joys, agonies, victories and losses that stood between me now and that last moment right here so long ago stretched out like the vast, black distances of the universe. Yet I knew there was a connection and I was closing a circle that was my life to this one poignant moment.

I strode to the stairs and climbed them easily. As a child I ponderously laboured from one rough plank to the next, sometimes terrified to ascend or descend but finally rising triumphant into the exotic ambience of the hayloft where sunlight streamed into the dust-laden air through gaps in the vertical siding boards. Clearly the loft had been long-empty and I was disconcerted to realize how much smaller it was than in my cathedral-sized memory. Yet the building was indeed massive, even to adult perceptions. Reverting to the perspective of the small boy that I once was, the scale of my memory became accurate. I was awe-struck to discover that the entire upper portion of the barn was framed with huge, clear, solid oak timbers. All were square-hewn, the marks of broad-axe and adze clearly visible. I wondered how long it had been since oak trees large enough to produce such timbers had grown in the area, and I speculated that the barn must be at least one hundred years old. All the framing was joined with mortise and tendon joints which were in turn secured with hardwood pegs. Not one steel nail helped secure any of the structural components.

I kicked at the remaining mouldy hay and remembered jumping from the upper beams into sweet fresh alfalfa below that had once filled the barn almost to the top rafters. I stood by the huge sliding doors to the ramp outside where hay wagons once rolled directly into the loft, and I reminisced for a long while, my thoughts wafting away with the cooing and fluttering of the pigeons nesting in the rafters. Finally jarring myself from my reveries, I walked slowly from the barn and up the lane to my vehicle, looking back one last time, grateful that I had taken the morning to find this place again. It confirmed so many vivid memories that I had long suspected of being only fantastic inventions. There was tremendous value in that for me and I wanted to go back to the hospital to share the magic of the morning with my father. But how did you do that with someone you had said good-bye to for a final time, committing them to die without you? There was no going back. 'As if there ever was,' I thought bitterly, 'Oh Christ, pop, you miserable old fart, there was so much we never did together.' Again I wept, so alone in time and distance from anyone or anything to cling to, wandering desperately through the echoing hallways of my haunted memories, trying to find meaning or purpose for all of the pain and the lost moments of joy. 'But that is life,' I consoled myself, 'nothing but dead-ends and unanswered questions. It is no different for anyone else, even if you choose to see yourself as a freak. Do you really think you have a monopoly on misery? Now get on with your day.' I drove out onto the highway and headed for Palermo Corners.

I stopped there to admire the buildings that stood unchanged, exactly as I remembered them. It was comforting to have my memories repeatedly confirmed. The day was becoming an orgy of recollection, verification and absolution. It was a comfort to be able to prove to myself that what I cast my mind back upon had actually once happened and existed. I felt vindicated and finally exonerated from much of the pain and guilt I had carried all my life. My memories had seemed too strange and bizarre to be anything more than fabrications that I had invented for inexplicable reasons. I had needed to prove that they were real, not the product of a sick imagination. I was slowly accepting the idea that it was not my fault that life had gone as it had and in fact, considering the circumstances of my existence, I had found rationality and meaning despite all the madness that formed part of my pathetic legacy. That was an achievement. I had reason to feel honourable. Although for the moment I was exhausted, I knew I could recoup my strength and rise above my self-imposed limits and inhibitions. A gentle peace and a sense of hope settled on me as I walked around the old buildings at the junction of the highways. It was, I decided, something that people often call *'closure'*.

Palermo held several memories for me but its true significance was that it had essentially been a hub of my life. Through this point my family had repeatedly travelled on its incessant peregrinations between jobs and farms. There had been a time when we had travelled regularly to go to church in Milton, a twenty-five mile drive each way from our home in Oakville, sometimes twice on Sundays. Why we did that I did not know. My parents were continually realigning their affinity from one evangelical church and denomination to another. They never bonded anywhere, never developed a sense of community and seemed afraid to develop any lasting allegiance or commitment. Oddly they each seemed to hope that they would make friendships during our meanderings. They migrated helter-skelter to visit people who were solid, rational citizens, steadfast and reliable, a very different type of personality from that of my parents. Yet my parents never seemed to stop trying to emulate the characters that perhaps they wanted to become. Forty years later, they still maintained contact with some of these same people. As a child I felt that these friendships were often formed out of pity and a sense of Christian duty towards us. Horrified, I realized that because of my insecure nature, I had often appealed to others' sympathy in an effort to gain their attention and affection. Pity me hire me, pity me make love to me, pity me reward me for being pathetic. Did I still do it? The thought appalled me.

Turning north, I proceeded toward Milton. The road stretched ahead of me flat and straight across the gently rolling farmland. In the distance to the northwest rose the ramparts of the Niagara Escarpment, a distinct barrier in the landscape running for many miles to the north. The scenery was punctuated regularly by gullies and undulating copses of hardwood. I imagined this area before the Europeans came as one massive forest with towering oak, elm, birch and maple. The pine and spruce would have been massive as well. Beneath the trees' luxuriant canopies large herds of deer roamed unmolested. Wolves and bear had also thickly populated the area along with several other indigenous species that were now gone or nearly extinct. It was a hard land to conquer with fierce long winters, rugged terrain and nothing but determination, hand labour and brute force to overcome the odds. Now the land was tamed, organized, urbanized and industrialized. Even the farmland, so hard-won, had become only space for more development. I wondered how it was possible to have a burgeoning population with a steadily less visible means of feeding it.

Rural southern Ontario as I had known it no longer existed. When I was young, people were still able to make a living from mixed farming. Each farm supported at least a few families and most holdings passed from generation to generation. There was a sense of stability to life. People expected the world they lived in to be the same one where they would raise their children. People were confident that they possessed all the skills needed to pass on to their children, just as their parents had done before them. Often three or even four generations resided on the same farm, perhaps under the same roof. There was a sense of permanence and continuity, of nurturing and mutual interest in one another's well-being. Expectation levels were lower and generally everyone seemed content. Families were larger and houses were smaller, with few of the luxuries that everyone now regards as essential. Even in town, homes were often heated with wood or coal and many had their own wells; city water systems were optional. Children shared bedrooms, one for the boys, one for the girls and there was only one bathroom if there was one at all. It was not unthinkable to have an outhouse in the backyard, somewhere beyond the vegetable garden. There was no angst about where to put the pool or the hot tub or the outdoor sound system. Other than the family dog, there were no security systems and little need for them. In my lifetime of almost a half-century, I realized that the world as I had known it was completely altered, gone forever with only a few fragments from the past still lingering. Now change occurs for its own sake. Few seem to remember or care where they have come from and have no idea of where they are going. Our world is now evolving so rapidly that no-one can clearly see the future. It is out of control, a contagious madness of acquisition and accumulation. Often it is all a facade. I wonder how people endure the daily pressure of a hyper existence without question or reflection. Like demented drones, our sole reason to be is to consume as much as possible. I try to maintain awareness of these things and yet still battle with myself about what is worth pursuing and what should be ignored. 'Values and prices,' I muse, 'are two different things. So many people pay such a high price for a life with so little value.'

Happily, I recognized the same old landmarks, a bridge here, a farm there, even certain trees still stood as I had known them so many years ago. I told myself to absorb as much as I could as I may never be back again, or, everything may be gone the next time. I drove across the arched concrete bridge that crossed the sixteen mile creek as it meanders its way north to Milton. An old cinder-block garage stood as it had during my childhood, still open for business, with a faded 'White Rose Gasoline' sign creaking in the wind. The further I drove away from the urban fringe along Lake Ontario, the more I realized the sense of permanence that I longed for. Once I drove into Milton I was elated to find the old town essentially unchanged, most of the surrounding farmland still functioning as it always had, the streets of the town familiar and welcoming. The only visible differences were the modern vehicles on the streets and that on the main street, and the fact that cars no longer angle-parked along its centre. When I was a child, cars had been huge and most lacked power steering, making parallel parking was very difficult. The same old trees, yet leafless in the early spring, formed a canopy over the streets. The small but well cared-for homes appeared just as they had when I was a child. Rather than the service and commercial centre it had once been, Milton was now a sleepy little agricultural town, functioning mainly as a dormitory community for Toronto, minutes away on a modern freeway. Still its farm-town character persisted, the quintessential southern Ontario hinterland community.

I stopped for lunch in the 'Waltzing Weasel Pub' located in an old hotel on the main street. The last time I had passed here I was still too young to legally enter any pub. I drove around the town, stunned to recognize many small points of interest, houses, even particular trees, and to remember people and their names. The larger homes were built of brick, cinderblock or sandstone; most of the smaller ones were of wood -frame construction. Many of these smaller houses had been modernized with vinyl siding but several still retained their original shingle or brick coverings. The small houses were appealing, seeming to make a statement that defied the concept of 'more is best'. They represented a quiet sense of security that said, 'This is all I need. I have nothing to prove by trying to make an impression.' It was delightful to see that all these small homes were well maintained, displaying pride and dignity, the owners apparently content with what they had.

In the middle of the town core stood the massive and imposing granite walls of the former Halton County Jail. My father had worked here as a guard when I was born and I recalled a photograph of my mother, and my father dressed in his guard's uniform, posing with me in a studio. I could not have been more than a few months old when the photo had been made. My father told me stories about butchering road-killed deer brought in the night for meat in the prison kitchen, and there were accounts of blasting unruly prisoners in their cell with a fire hose. It would have been the sort of job he loved, the uniform, the authority, the control, the sense of being able to punish, and I wondered what had happened that he had gone back to work on the farms. I suspected it had something to do with his temper and his penchant for inappropriate behaviour. The prison still stood, imposing as ever, but now used for administrative offices. On one side it faced a park graced with immaculately maintained gardens, a large band shell and several ancient wheeled cannon, relics from wars that local citizens had fought in. A war memorial with its bronze soldier posed in grim determination with rifle and bayonet, glared down on a children's playground. Passing along each side of the park and continuing along the prison walls, the streets ran in perfect squares. One was named King Street. Suddenly I paused in startled reverie.

King Street was strangely significant. I recalled that this was where we had lived when we moved into Milton from a house in an outlying village during a very hard winter. We had been 'frozen out' as my mother had described it. We had rented a tiny house on this street. I wondered if I would recognize it, if it still stood. After careful observation I was sure I had found it, and was overwhelmed with a strange emotion. I had a sense of 'déjà vu' and then realized that this must be the exact spot of which I held a recurring memory.

The image was soft, like a copy of an old photograph and I realized that it was probably a memory of a memory, but still it was easy enough to hear a horse's hoofs clopping in the quiet of early morning. The first light of dawn filtered through the canopy of chlorophyll-green leaves of the trees that lined this street. It must have been spring and if it was, I could not have been more than one year old! Impossible! The horse drew a milkman's wagon as it slowly plodded up the street, stopping at intervals of its own accord, waiting for the milkman to catch up and reload his wire basket with more glass bottles. The milkman wore a white uniform and cap; faintly, I imagined I could still hear the clink of the milk bottles. I recalled reading a story where the milkman's horse had been trained to advance only when the bottles were jingled in a certain way.

'What a mundane thing to retain as a first memory,' I thought, but the image was indelible and a soothing peaceful recollection. 'This is the street, this is the place!' I could hardly contain my sense of amazement, and fought the urge to go and knock on the door of the little house. I smiled as I imagined trying to explain why I had called on a perfect stranger to share my moment within the circles of time.

I remembered someone called Grandma Prudholm, her fresh muffins and a large flower-filled garden. A smiling old lady who lived alone, she was a friend of my mother's. There were so many little pieces of memories like this that I could not fit together, but it did not matter. When my daughter was young, we would go for walks along the beach and she would excitedly gather pretty pebbles and bits of broken, coloured glass. They were collected in her hat and taken home to add to her collection of treasures. Now I visualized these fragments of happy memory as being like those fragmented pieces of smoothed, old multi-coloured bottles, knowing that at one time they had held something of significance. It is said that a whole is the sum of its parts; I treasured these molecules of happiness and savoured the moment, committing even that precious feeling to my own hat filling with recollections.

Two blocks further along, on Robert's Street, I came upon the Zimmerman house, another central point in my young life, the metal number seventy four still nailed on the front porch. This was the house where my parents had met as boarders; perhaps I had even been conceived here! My parents had remained friends of that family for many years and in fact, I knew that my mother remained in contact with the old lady who was yet alive, now in her mid-nineties. I recalled Thanksgiving and New Year turkey dinners I had eaten here. The whole huge traditional meal, a monstrous carved turkey complete with cranberries, mountains of mashed potatoes, bowls of gravy, yams, mashed turnips, puddings, mincemeat tarts, and pumpkin pies. The meals always ended with the agony of having eaten far too much, but it seemed that children were expected to eat until they were ill, then castigated for having a small appetite. After the meal, bowls of candy and sweet pastries were insistently offered to the agonized guests. The old man, Elmer, was a German bricklayer who took great delight entertaining me. He could spend hours telling stories and delighted in tickling me, exactly what an overfed child needed. I remember him paring pieces from a block of chewing tobacco and spitting the blood-red juice into the wood stove in a back kitchen. The back yard was filled with a bricklayer's paraphernalia and I enjoyed playing among the cement mixers, carts and trolleys that lay there. So impossibly long ago, these vignettes seemed liked faded clips from someone else's home movie.

I drove past the fair grounds where the town annually hosts a 'Steam Show'. Antique, steam-powered agricultural equipment is brought together for a working exhibition. It was an event that delighted my father and I had been brought here several times. Nearby was yet another church the family had attended for a while. As a youngster I was often taken from the church service, spanked severely for something I had innocently done, and then left alone in the old Ford car until my parents were ready to leave for home. I would cry myself to sleep in the stuffy car interior many times; the smell of old car upholstery came to mind. The church was located on the bank of the Sixteen Mile Creek which ran through the centre of town. A short distance away was the home of the pastor's family who had fostered me during one of the times when there had been an upheaval between my parents. There was a small boy about my age in this family. One day he had slid down the steep bank of the stream and ended up crouching in a tree that hung over the rushing water. I ran for help and was later credited with saving the life of the family's only child. I had seized the moment and appealed to live permanently with this family but neither they, nor I, had a choice about that and once again I went back to the same sorry home. Another insignificant memory on its own, I filed it with the other broken bits in the hat. Perhaps it would later prove to be of value.

I drove around and through the town a last time, savouring the feeling I found here, and then drove away on a back road, in pursuit of more memories. I passed a turnoff for a place called Rattlesnake Point. It was a vantage point on the escarpment that provided a view for several miles. Once I had frequented this place. It had a steep winding road that wound up the face of the escarpment. When I first started driving, I delighted in coming here. There were several caves in the face of the escarpment and I had found a strange pleasure in crawling and clambering through the labyrinths. On one occasion, entirely alone I had tried to find a new cave and had become firmly stuck while trying to crawl through a narrow gap, remaining there for several hours in the total blackness. With no light, nobody knowing I was there, the weight of the entire planet seeming to crush down on me. I had struggled desperately in a wild panic, until finally exhausted I had fallen asleep. Thus relaxed, I was able to wiggle free of my confines and emerged again into the failing light of day. I tensed at the memory and wondered what had possessed me to do such things. What security was I seeking in the bowels of the earth?

Now I came to a corner with a road sign pointing to Kilbride, the first place I had lived after being born. I turned onto the winding road with a growing anticipation. I had fond memories of this place, especially of the water-powered mill that had still been a functioning enterprise when I was last here in the mid-sixties. It was powered by a huge undershoot wheel, the stream running beneath the wheel and it was amazing to realise the amount of energy harnessed from one small rushing body of water. Inside the mill a massive wooden shaft had run the entire length of the building. Crude sub-shafts were powered from it by means of interlocking hardwood spokes arranged at ninety degrees to the primary angle of rotation. All these shafts were carried in large leather bearings that were oiled regularly. There was a soft, rhythmic creaking and groaning throughout the large wooden building as the machinery turned incessantly. Pulleys of various diameters were attached along the shafts and on these rode large, flapping belts that drove the individual pieces of machinery. The belts were necessarily loose so that they could be slid on and off the different-sized pulleys to start and stop the machinery and adjust their speeds. To prevent the belts from whipping and slapping excessively, each one was installed with a half-twist in it and they were moved on and off the drive-pulleys with long forked wooden sticks. The mill was a wonder to see in motion, elegantly simply and, although crude by modern standards, it was efficient and cost effective.

The mill generated its own electricity but its main function was that of a grist mill. Local farmers brought their various grains to be ground into flour and meal. The inside of the place was coated in fine dry flour everywhere and the risk of fire must have been tremendous. On one side of the mill was a machine shop, its various lathes and drills powered from the main shaft, and I seem to remember an attached blacksmith forge. On the far end was a small sawmill that turned local timber into lumber as required by the surrounding farms and homes. Older men in caps and bib-overalls worked there; it had been a social centre for the locals who gathered there in commercial exchange and male camaraderie. The mill was an ultimate statement about self-sufficiency and communal interdependence. The tiny village had probably developed around its existence. I was excited at the prospect of seeing it once again and wondered if it still functioned as an independent business or was now a novel tourist attraction. I dreaded that it may have been converted to a trendy restaurant or a cluster of boutiques.

I travelled down to the gully through which ran the stream to the mill then, winding up the other side, I presently came to the heart of the village. It was virtually unchanged! Amazingly, the old general store still stood and was open for business. It had once been named 'Johnstone's Store' but although the name was new, everything seemed perfectly preserved including the same, large tin signs advertising soft drinks as they had in the early fifties. Across the street lay the old graveyard and on the other corner the gas station, although renovated, was still in business. To one side of the store the old church still stood and it also appeared still to be doing business. At the back of the store an ancient cement trough held the spring water that yet gurgled bright and clear from a huge cast iron pipe that had hooks to hang pails as they were filled. Presumably it was the spring that had determined the location of the village. I tried to imagine a time when local residents came to this well to collect all their domestic water, carrying it home winter and summer, night and day as required. Horses drank here at one time and all the community once relied on the one simple unifying source of water. Most of the small homes in the village still had large stacks of firewood, clothes lines, dog houses, and dirt driveways. Little was different from when I had last been here thirty years earlier. The village was still perfectly quaint.

Parking the car, I climbed the bare wooden steps to a long veranda that ran along the front of the store. Its posts were still decorated with the same wooden ginger-bread that I was there when I was an infant. I used to come here during hot summer evenings with my parents for ice cream and soda -pop. Entering the store, I was stunned to recognize the very same old Pepsi bottle cooler inside the front door where it had always sat.   The floor was still covered with heavy checkerboard linoleum, which also looked original. On one side of the store, shelves groaned with the weight of home baking, pies, cookies, bread, and there were rows of home preserves, fruit, vegetables, jams, and jellies, all for sale. A young girl stood behind the counter and when I explained how long ago I had frequented this place and how excited I was to find it like this, she looked at me as if I were an alien. I suppose I was. I suddenly felt like a foolish old man, raving on about something that no-one else knew or cared about. I had never had a sense of my own antiquity before and, although fleeting, it had a sobering effect. On inquiring about the mill, I was shattered to learn that it had burned down long ago. 'Years before I was born anyway,' said the girl, not appearing to have any regrets about something she had never known. My high emotion plummeted to a deep sadness.

I did not know how my parents had come to live in this tiny village, but for several years they had friends here named Gweny and Angus, who were possibly the connection. Gweny had a brother named Bucky Landeaux, a memorable character who wore thick glasses under a baseball cap always pulled down low over his face. To look at anyone he had to tilt his head back and peer along his nose. He sported a mouthful of buck teeth, hence his name, and he looked like a cartoon rodent. He drove a huge green car that was raised in the front, had fender skirts, long radio aerials with racoon tails tied to the ends, and was always blowing a weird, loud horn. Around the window hung a string of small red and white pompons, and at night a row of green and purple 'sex lights' (as they were called)) glowed between them. On the hood a naked chrome nymph lay into the wind spreading her red plastic wings. Bucky would peer under his cap up over the elevated hood of the car, revving the engine that roared through his 'Hollywood' mufflers and would race back and forth along the half-block main street of the village squealing his tires and trying to be the image of a rebel. 'Well, Bucky old boy, where are you now?' I mused, 'Every village needs its idiot and I won't be here long enough to get on steady.'

Two doors down from the store I located the house where we must have lived; I faintly recognized it from photographs I had seen. We had been here for at least part of one winter. I knew that my father worked as a prison guard while we were here. I had heard the stories about how I would awaken and quietly tie my father's boot laces into impossible knots while he prepared breakfast early in the morning before going to work. My father then drove an ancient Ford Model 'A' with a folding black top. I vaguely remember a cream-coloured car with large, narrow-spoked wheels and huge pod headlights. Dad had told me that I would be delighted when he retarded the manual engine timing and made it backfire. 'Car model A, putt, putt bang!', was apparently what I called the car. I remember that my father had once swerved to miss something and the car had careened into the ditch on its side. I had been riding in the backseat with a family friend, Madeline Zimmerman, and we lay buried for a few moments in the week's groceries which had toppled on top of us. There was raucous laughter once it was realized no-one was injured. 'Another insignificant event,' I thought, 'How do I remember something as irrelevant as that?' but I filed it away in the pile that was slowly building.

This is where a photo had been taken of me in my winter snow-suit, standing waist-deep in the snow of the front yard of that house pointing up at the sky. I had been told that I was watching RCAF Vampire fighter jets and that 'pet pane' was one of my first words. Clink and tinkle into the pile went yet another insignificant shard; it was becoming an interesting collection.

I drove south from the village through an area known as Cedar Springs and along a winding road that eventually led back to the Dundas Highway, where it passed through the small community of Waterdown. My mother had acquired a small cabin at a Pentecostal church camp near Paris and this was halfway along the route from Oakville to that place. Driving through the town admiring its apparent reluctance to change, I was jarred with the memory of an event that I had completely forgotten until that moment.

For several years after moving to the half-acre in town that my father had rented, there was a large vacant lot next door. It held an old house and a small cabin but the rest of the property was wild and overgrown. There was a large population of wild rabbits which Dad regarded as a personal threat to his gardening efforts. There was also an ongoing plague of racoons in the area, invading garbage cans and creating a nuisance, especially to a character like my father who loved to turn anything into a drama. The man also held an illusion that people were constantly trying to steal produce from his garden so he came to the astute conclusion that he needed to defend his holdings - with an air rifle! He diligently set about decimating the local rabbit population and I was soon well educated in how to kill and dress a rabbit for the stew pot. One day a large old racoon was spotted high in an elm tree in the neighbouring property. It had done nothing wrong, but it was something new to try and kill. Dad fired at it several times with the air rifle until the old creature leapt out of the tree, falling to his death. Close inspection of the vermin-infested corpse revealed a tiny pellet hole in one ear, the suspected cause of its fatal plunge. It was a story my father revelled in telling. Some men bragged about the huge buck deer they had bagged. My father had his racoon story. The rifle was kept over the kitchen door, just like in a frontier cabin in a western film, ready for immediate use whenever a furry threat arose.

By the age of eight I was continually depressed and desperate, to the point of considering extreme measures, including suicide. There seemed to be nowhere and no one to turn to. It is a terrible thing for a child to be overwhelmed with that sense of absolute hopelessness. This feeling is a recurring curse that I have carried through my entire life. I can never comprehend why as a boy I had to carry such a weight of desperation. There was no joy or peace in my life. I had no friends. My parents fought constantly and, despite repeated incidents involving police, social workers and people from various churches, life was a dreary repetition of the same black routines. Everything seemed to be a dead end. Hopelessness is not something a child should ever have to feel in any culture.

I schemed for a way out and decided to leave home but was not sure of where to go. Finally I decided that I would try to find my way to a farm belonging to friends of my parents. Perhaps I could persuade their son to help me while I hid out in their barn and decided what to do next. Maybe I could live in the hay loft for the winter. It was a feeble scheme, but it was a plan and with that comes hope and, with hope, a reason for living. That farm was almost fifty miles away; I reckoned that it would take me three or four days to make my way there. I carefully filled a pack with some food and the few items I felt were necessary. One autumn morning I made my move. I waited until my father had left for work, which was long before my mother would rise. I took the air rifle and was gone in the dim light of early morning. There was about a mile of open going through the streets of town until I could make my way into the deep, wooded valley of Sixteen Mile Creek. I reasoned boyishly that if I were to be followed it would be more difficult if I waded across the creek, which I did at each shallow place I found. The day wore on and I made my way along deer trails until finally I came to my beloved woodlot near the back of the old Lingren farm.

I stopped and made a small fire to warm myself and heat a can of beans. It was a crisp, bright autumn day and I realized that it would be a cold night. I would have to find shelter. I also realized that, if anyone should be looking for me, this area may well be one of the first places searched so I decided to press on into the remains of the day, hoping for the best. I climbed up the steep, high creek bank and made my way to the highway on the west side of the bridge over the creek. The only route I knew for the next few miles was along the highway. I plodded along for a while trying to thumb a ride from passing vehicles. Eventually an old man in an ancient truck stopped and took me as far as Waterdown, letting me off just as we reached the edge of town.

This meant that I had to walk a gauntlet along the highway that was also the main street through town. It was now late afternoon and getting colder with the gathering darkness. I fought a rising panic but knew I had no choice but to soldier on. There was no thought of turning back. I had resolved there was nothing to go back for. I managed to go only a few blocks before being stopped by a passing policeman. My adventure was over, not even a full day into the gambit.

It was the air rifle that had attracted the officer's attention. I soon found myself in the warmth and brightness of the police station where I was interrogated about who I was, where I was from and where I was going with a firearm. I kept replying that it was only an air rifle and would not give them any other information. I felt that I was a desperado and a fugitive and sincerely did not want to go home preferring, even hoping, that they would lock me in a jail cell.

Finally the officers searched through my packsack and found some identification. Despite my pleading they promptly telephoned my home, and father was on his way to the police station. I feared the worst and waited in trepidation for my father's arrival. When he arrived, the police lectured my father about leaving the air rifle where I had had access to it and then sent us on our way. There was never a question about why I had done what I had, if I intended to do it again, or how I had managed to cover so much distance in a single day. Instead of being angry, dad seemed proud of what I had done, as if it were a major achievement. 'I can see you're a chip off the old block,' he declared proudly. He said that he understood how my mother had driven me to do it. There was no point in trying to tell him that far more than mother had motivated me. I was happy enough to know I would not be beaten, and I was not going to jeopardize the situation. For weeks after my parents continued to rage on at each other about that day, each claiming the other to be the reason I had run away. They would not understand that I had not been trying to make a statement. I had actually been trying to get away from *them*. Ultimately nothing changed. Now as I drove through the town, I mused that I was still running. One of my favourite songs, Bob Seger's 'Against the Wind' happened to begin to play on the car radio just then and I sang along with the music: 'Living to run, running to live, still running against the wind'.

The road stretched out ahead of me, pleasantly undulating through rolling farmland and quaint little villages with old-world names like Aberfoyle, Glen Morris, or

Braeside. It was about forty miles from the family home in Oakville to the church camp, which had been an annual expedition. A week before we left to spend part of the summer at the camp dad would arrange for the car to be serviced and tuned-up. It was incredible that he could make an ordeal out of travelling a distance that should be no more than an hour's drive; but then it did seem to take us all day to get there. I could not remember what took us so long but it was a ridiculous journey. The car would be packed the night before. Everyone would rise extra early, breakfast, complete final preparations and then sally forth with a 'wagons ho' grim determination - Braeside Camp or bust. Most families would not make as much fuss over a motor trip across the entire continent. Perhaps the simple drive was turned into an ordeal because a forty mile drive in England might be considered a grand journey and my English father continued the tradition. The simple truth is, however, that both my parents had a penchant for making a big deal out of nothing at all.

As we drove along my father took delight in announcing the place name of each landmark no matter how insignificant, as well as the next name upcoming. 'Waterdown! Waterdown! Aberfoyle next!' It was tiresome and embarrassing, especially when he would roll down the window and make animal sounds at the livestock standing in the passing fields. Mother would begin to fuss about what she thought she had forgotten to bring along, and complained fiercely if anyone opened a window to relieve the stifling heat or the stench of a fart.

Flatulence was one thing guaranteed to draw a sense of merriment from my parents, although at times mother would berate father for an especially odoriferous emission. It seemed that the old man could fart at will. I had once joked that he could probably blast out God Save the Queen. 'It takes a good horse to fart at the end of the day,' he would declare proudly as he trumpeted yet another greasy, foul rendition. His other witticism about farting and horses was that 'a farting horse will never tire; a farting man's the one to hire!' Perhaps all the flatulence was a result of poor diet, but I am clearly my parent's son in this regard. I have farted my way through school, through my working career, through amorous encounters, (some which ended abruptly), in crowded elevators, while piloting tiny aircraft shoulder to shoulder with my passengers, in swimming pools and bathtubs, at the desks of clients while tending to critical business, at my own wedding (and others' too), in busy restaurants, and even while being fitted for a new suit. My posterior aspirations seem as normal and automatic a bodily function as breathing or yawning. It is part of my heritage, a legacy and a birthright. There was a medieval belief that flatulence was directly related to madness and perhaps there is some weight to the notion. I often wonder what it is about breaking wind that is so often hilarious to many people. If flatulence is good reason for mirth, if humour were currency, then I would never be broke. No pun intended.

Somewhere along the way we would stop for a picnic, sitting at some roadside turnout eating warm, soggy sandwiches and warm, thin Koolaid. Then we would drive off the paved highway, onto the dusty, gravel country back roads that would take us circuitously toward the camp. Eventually we would arrive at our cabin. It was actually just a small shack which mother had bought for forty dollars but, crude as it was, she had a sense of owning some sort of home. More hours would go by while the cabin was inspected, opened up, aired and cleaned. Each window had a huge shutter hinged along the top which was lifted up and propped in place. Ostensibly the shutters were to prevent intruders during most of the year when the cabin was vacant, but all they did was make the little hut look like some sort of ridiculous fortress. They also had a way of dropping with a crash in the middle of the night.

The camp was a bizarre place. It belonged to a Pentecostal church organization and was run as a business. Mother paid a lease fee annually for the space the cabin occupied. There were numerous 'owned' cabins and as many more that people rented. There were also dormitories where people could stay, as well as an area for people to park trailers and pitch tents. The entire summer community of shacks and shanties was built around a huge clapboard hall where evangelical church meetings were held every day from early morning till late at night. There was also a huge communal kitchen where people could eat. Beside it was a small store selling sundry treats and blocks of ice for the iceboxes in the cabins. Huge water tanks stood where people would come to fill buckets with horrible, sulphur-flavoured water which they packed back to their cabins. Several outhouses and communal washrooms were located randomly and a farm, which the camp also owned, was located adjacent to the camp. The farm, although ramshackle and certainly neither profitable nor complimentary to the camp, was the pride of its founder and manager, a sheep-faced old evangelist everyone lovingly referred to as Brother Blair.

Cows regularly found their way into the camp, which was encircled with a complex network of dirt lanes. These were sprinkled with a sticky calcium mixture to keep dust levels minimal. People outfitted in their go-to-church finery tiptoed through the mud, dust and cow shit and past reeking garbage barrels to attend the various ongoing spiritual activities. The scheme was to saturate everyone in a Pentecostal hellfire and salvation environment, holy ghost weirdness, miracle healing and general 'Christian' fun time, that was intended to indoctrinate people en masse and extract as much of their cash as possible. A huge bell above the kitchen was rung regularly through the day to announce various meetings and mealtimes. At night it would clang out a curfew when children were all supposed to be indoors. I had never enjoyed any of it much and preferred to call the place 'Stalag Jesus'.

In contradiction to that which was holy, chaste and pure in thought and deed, there was also a counter culture at the camp that came to drink, smoke, party and get laid. It seemed that there was a strange sort of deception in place, a blind double standard. Most of the adult pilgrims did not notice the antithesis in their midst, the army of Lucifer in their camp. Probably they were just too naive to comprehend what else took place on hallowed ground. Their daughters wore socks to their knees and dresses to their ankles but that did not mean that they had a diminished interest in fornication and being 'evil'. After all, you had to be a sinner before you could be saved. One of the delights of being saved was to be able to 'give testimony' about the sin and corruption you had been redeemed from. Maybe it was part of the apprenticeship of the Born Again.

The camp was also subject to occasional night time raids by motorcycle gangs. The camp's men folk ran after them frantically while the women prayed furiously inside their shuttered cabins. The bikers careened around the camp making as much racket as possible with roaring engines, breaking bottles, shouts and jeers. Some would race around the shanty community with naked girlfriends riding perilously on the back of the motorcycles. There was a strange ebb and flood of good and evil and the evangelists capitalized on any shenanigans as proof that the evil one was always among them and that everyone desperately needed salvation and saturation in the mysterious 'Holy Ghost'. I saw it all then, and now, as a farcical sham designed to exploit people. Even as a child, I was cynical about religion. Nevertheless, I at one time pretended to subscribe to the zealous doctrines in an attempt to please my mother. It didn't work and I was left with an indelible impression about how ridiculous it all seemed to be.

I would break away from the camp on my own as often as possible, crossing the road and descending a steep bank to the railway tracks that ran along the banks of the Grand River. Sometimes I would walk the two miles into Paris, downstream from the camp. Most often I would go fishing, catching small, muddy-tasting bass at various spots along the river bank. How I savoured the hot, lazy afternoons and the sweet reek of creosote from the railway ties! I would throw handfuls of crushed rock through the telegraph wires beside the tracks and listen to the delightful pinging sound. I explored the surrounded hills and found an abandoned kiln, long overgrown and another railway, abandoned with tracks removed, but leading to a set of empty bridge pylons crossing the river. The hot summer afternoons were heavy with the scent of wildflowers and fresh-mown hay, and the hypnotic clatter of cicadas and grasshoppers. It was a mysterious piece of country which, it seemed, I had all to myself. I savour my memories of those summer afternoons when I roamed alone and free through the fields and open hills.

When I was older I was hired as a summer assistant to the full-time caretaker who lived there. I collected the garbage, cleaned washrooms, cleared brush, kept the communal water tanks pumped full from the underground well, and worked at various ongoing painting and maintenance projects. I also helped on the adjacent farm with haying and tending the livestock. It was an idyllic way for a boy to spend his summers and learn new skills away from the twin clouds of madness that were my parents. I boarded with the caretaker's family who had a son the same age. In the evenings we would take our .22 rifles and hunt groundhogs, wandering the hills behind the camp and farm. Sometimes we were able to coax girls from the camp to visit the barn with us where we would play out the eternal drama of young adults alone in a hay loft. Our conversations were filled with the speculations of normal adolescent boys obsessed with sex, cars, perceived symbols of manhood, and the bafflements of our raging teenage chemistry. I drove the tractors and the camp vehicles, worked like a man, sweating and swaggering, suddenly possessing a sense of self-worth and promise that I had never known before. It was probably the one time in my youth when I enjoyed a few brief weeks of being normal. Then tragically, I would have to return to my real life.

That afternoon I drove the roads of the countryside savouring the gentle, pastoral scenery and basking in the happy memories. I admired the ancient stone fences and granite-block houses built by early Scottish settlers and the red brick homes built by the English. I revelled in the sense of peaceful permanence that I felt in this place, wishing I could capture it and take it home. In the small, quaint village of Glen Morris I turned back toward Paris, so that I could drive by the church camp and continue my circuitous passage through old haunts. Finally I passed the camp and was shocked to see that it had doubled in size. The farm was gone, completely overrun by a rambling trailer park. There were new buildings everywhere. I drove by without stopping, disillusioned that sprawling development had been openly adopted by the fundamentalists. I considered that mindlessness was the greatest asset within their dogma. Obviously, growth and profit had risen to a higher value than country charm and quaint, rustic Christian retreat.

In a few minutes I had driven into Paris, a picturesque textile and mill town built of stone and brick that hung over the banks of the Grand River. It had been very prosperous at one time but now there was a sense of regression and decay to the community. It was a lovely, peaceful place over-endowed with churches, formerly grandiose houses, and a short main street which seemed to have all the same businesses still faltering along as they had so many years before. A pub on the riverbank advertised a wake that evening, 'Everyone welcome. Admission $10'.

I drove toward Brantford, a large industrial town a few miles downstream on the river, once another appealing community. It still possessed a faded beauty but there was an appearance of abandonment and poverty; many businesses were closed or obviously struggling. I was saddened to realize that small-town southern Ontario was falling before the unchecked growth of larger urban centres and the cancerous spread of modern subdivisions. I drove back toward Oakville through Ancaster and Hamilton. A sense of weary disillusionment fell on me as I drove through these squalid, dreary towns. I had been born here, but could not summon the interest or energy to explore the city. To my eyes, it was a depressing industrial area, although I knew that Hamilton was culturally rich and possessed fine public gardens and grand architecture. Suddenly I felt that I had seen enough. I was exhausted and just wanted to go home to British Columbia. 'A nice place to visit,' I thought, 'perhaps I'll come again in another twenty-six years. It's as good a place as any to be from.'

I drove back into Oakville and left the vehicle at the old house for Helen. I walked down the long laneway, pausing to look back one last time. I longed to find one more happy memory, something so good that it justified and even diminished all the dreary unhappiness, the rage and violence, the ignorance and alienation. I could not. There were memories that I tried to push aside, but standing there I confronted them, deciding that if I could not find warm, happy memories then I may as well deal with the ugly realities that demanded recognition once and for all, and then get on with living.

My parents had fought incessantly and violently. Both possessed an irrational rage that was satiated only when they exhausted their frenzied outbursts on whoever or whatever stood in their path. They were as indiscriminate as a tornado mindlessly carving a trail of destruction. I had even been awaked more than once by being dragged from my bed and beaten for something I had allegedly done. For the rest of my life I will have difficulty sleeping soundly, and am paranoid about being surprised by anyone who stealthily approaches me from behind.

Near the end of my parent's marriage, the violence escalated. One Sunday morning while the family sat at breakfast, yet another altercation broke out. My father later claimed that my mother had reached for a butcher knife. All I remember is that suddenly my father had picked up the entire table with breakfast upon it, and slammed it upside down to the floor, my mother underneath. She was then thrown against the kitchen cabinets. Her head was severely gashed, blood streaming down her face and scalp, mixing with the food on the floor. I still see the shattered sugar bowl lying on the floor, its contents soaking up the dark red stain, and I hear my mother screeching hideously. Police, ambulances, the usual routine, my father in jail, the uneasy dark period of brooding, silent tension in the days that followed, the weary repetitive pattern worked itself out once again, except that this time, it was the beginning of the end. Finally!

My mother's rages and tantrums increased in degree and frequency. She was extremely volatile and completely unpredictable. One day without warning and certainly no provocation she flew into a berserk fury and seized my little sister, picking her up by one ear and flinging her hard against a wall. Ruth hit the wall with a sickening thud and slid down to the floor. Horrified, I had seen the assault and rushed into the room, bursting with adrenaline strength. I flung my mother to the floor screaming at her that if she moved, I would kill her. My fury stunned her and she cowered there, suddenly sobbing wildly as only she could. I tended to Ruth, amazingly uninjured, although dazed and disoriented, shattered more by the fact of the incident that the act itself. I comforted and reassured her and led her outside, telling her to wait there until I came back for her. Dragging my mother from the floor I slammed her against the wall, one hand around her throat, one raised in a fist that hovered over her face and unleashed my frustration. 'You fucking stupid old bitch, that's your own daughter who you're throwing around like a dirty rag! What's the matter with you? If you have to do that then save for it for me. I can fight back. If you ever touch her like that again, I'll kill you!'

For the rest of my life the memory of those ugly minutes replays at times uncontrollably through my mind, over and over, unsolicited and dreaded. The same sick, dry feeling rises again in my throat. I am horrified at the uncontrollable rage which first possessed me that morning. I have known it all too often since that day. The realization that I too was infected with the same madness was even more horrifying than what my mother had done. I was thirteen years old at the time. My relationship with her was never the same again. I gave up trying to win her love and respect that day. We regarded each other with wary contempt and suspicion for the rest of our lives despite repeated attempts at reconciliation. She was afraid of me, and I of her and of what she might provoke me to do.

In the weeks that followed, my mother's tantrums did not diminish, but to my knowledge they were never again directed against my sister. Often when I returned home I would open the door to be greeted with a fusillade of shoes, pots and kitchen utensils, including knives that rattled off the wall around my head. I quietly accepted it, subdued by the shame of my threats against her, hoping that she would return to some degree of self control and stable behaviour. At night she would subject the family to hours of shouted prayer, beseeching God in a screaming voice to make the family see things her way, wailing horribly as she berated my father and me by asking God to punish us for our unfairness to her. As the sleepless nights continued, tensions rose, nerves frayed and the sense of hopelessness and impending doom increased like the rumbling of an approaching thunderstorm.

One day she was gone. She had taken Ruth and left, riding a bus all the way across the country to British Columbia. I worried horribly about my little sister, frustrated that there was nothing I could do for her. Yet I was relieved to be shed of my mother's tyranny and lunacy. As soon as I could, a few years later, I travelled west to see how my sister was faring and was appalled to confirm how my mother used and abused her, but there was little I could do to change anything. Ruth would marry immediately upon finishing high school to escape the continuing tyranny that our mother imposed on her. In turn the marriage turned out to be a dismal ordeal. Although Ruth immersed herself in the care of her several children, she had an unhappy, miserable existence, her husband a shiftless lout who had capitalized on her sad situation to procure a loyal and long-suffering wife.

The legacy of misery and senseless suffering continued into the next generation. Our aging mother demanded attention from Ruth, bitterly jealous of her marriage and children; she regarded her own grandchildren as competition for her daughter's attention. She alienated herself from both of us and our families, drove a second husband to the grave, (it was his only recourse), and lived alone, bitter at the world, never understanding that the sorrows she endured were entirely of her own making. She seemed to embrace misery as a virtue, all the while looking forward to an afterlife where she believed all would be bliss. She cheated herself and those who would love her of so much that is good.

Once mother left, I had only my father to deal with. At first it appeared that it was a new beginning and that life might improve but a few weeks later it had become clear that I was now only of nuisance value to my father. I was repeatedly accused of being 'just like your mother', an indictment that stung me bitterly. My mother had often claimed I was just like my father. My sense of being a pawn in the war between them led me to feeling deep guilt for the break-up of the family. More than once I was directly accused of being responsible for the failed marriage. At the same time my father revelled in his freedom from the tyranny of mother. Despite his religious inclinations took delight in getting drunk and fornicating as many women as possible. One day I came home and found my father with a huge black woman on the living room sofa, his hand jammed between her massive thighs. The way that he glared at me seemed a declaration that I was no longer welcome in my own home.

My father now directed all of his frustration against me, the violence escalated, the beatings and tirades were almost a daily ritual. Fortunately I was a burly boy for my years, hardened by the years of intense physical labour, and I was now well able to fend for myself bodily. Finally it all came to a head one day. My father was berating me about having joined the high-school wrestling team. 'So you think you're tough, eh boy? Well I was trained to kill with my bare hands and I'll hang a licking on you that you won't forget if you try getting cocky with me!' He had me backed into a corner and was ranting in my face. 'Look, Dad,' I pleaded, 'I haven't forgotten one beating you've ever given me. Please stop this bullshit once and for all!' 'Why you mouthy little bugger,' he roared, 'You've got a big, fat yap just like your bloody mother don't you?' He raised his fist and smashed me in the mouth.

Without thought or hesitation I grabbed him by the throat, my fingers closing around his larynx. Squeezing as hard as could, I raised my other hand. 'Well, you fucker, you blew your first shot, so here's a little of your own medicine back!' He was desperately grasping at my hand on his throat while I gave him a massive blow to his face. He crumpled like an old rag. I left him lying unconscious on the floor. 'Live by the sword, die by the sword, you prick!' I shouted at him as he lay there. Part of me hoped I had killed him and to this day I feel no remorse. I packed a few belongings and left. I was on my own, at barely the age of fourteen.

It was six weeks before I saw him again. He accosted me in a coffee shop. There were no queries about where I had been or how I was surviving. 'Cor, you hung a good one on me boy! Very nearly tore me throat out, couldn't talk for days! Wish I'd done that to my old man, maybe things would be different now.' He seemed to admire me for what I had done, yet there was a wall of animosity and neither of us offered apologies or suggestions of reconciliation. He offered a vague, mumbled offer, 'Come home when you want, you're free to come and go.' I seldom went home, only a few days or weeks now and then, but it never worked out. Our relationship never improved and we grew more distant as time went by.

I stood there in the driveway so many years later, bitter tears washing down my face. 'What a waste, a goddamned tragic fucking waste.' I was middle-aged and felt that my life had led nowhere, full of dead-ends and failures both personal and financial, a trail of painful and broken relationships, a litany of the sins of the fathers, and a hopeless struggle to overcome the dark madness that seemed to be my only legacy. It seemed that no matter how hard I tried otherwise, I emulated every foible of my parents. 'Perhaps this is the closure. Maybe I can get on with my life and make this trip a turning point. Maybe I can put all the shit behind me now than I can see that it isn't my fault. I don't need to keep on punishing myself for being a victim.' I tried to reason with myself, but I was too weary after the week I had endured. I turned and walked away down the driveway for the last time.

Slowly I strolled up the street past the houses and familiar things that were once part of my daily life. Everything seemed familiar and alien at the same time. I walked by an old stone house that had stood solidly for as long as I could remember. I was reminded of walking past it one hot summer day after my father had taken me on a long hike around half the county. I had been totally exhausted, each footstep a conscious effort, my throat and mouth burning dry. My father had been amused at my misery, with no concern for me. 'So now you know what I do for a living, how'd you like it then, heh?' 'Everything turned out like that with the old bastard,' I mused, 'He was always trying to prove something. He could never enjoy just being unless he was making someone else suffer. Damn it, why do I always find one more black memory. I came here looking for happy ones. Why can't I be like the kid that got locked in the barn for a week? He was happy as hell when they found him. Dug through the manure all week long, convinced that with all the shit there had to be a pony somewhere. Why can't I believe in a pony for once? Cheer the fuck up!'

I walked on past a row of tall apartment buildings, standing in what had once been a huge strawberry field. I had picked berries there once, fifty cents a flat, kneeling in the blazing sun, mouth puckered with all the warm berries I ate, fingers and lips stained red. I went home with two dollars for a day's hard work, and was told not to come back again if I was going to eat as much as I picked. I had suffered stomach cramps and diarrhoea half the night.

I followed the road across the Sixteen Mile Creek on a new bridge. When I had lived in Oakville and wanted to cross the creek it had been necessary to walk over the railway trestle that stood just beyond the new bridge. It did not look nearly as high as I remembered it, but then I was not standing on it now. It had seemed to be a mile long and a mile high, especially on a dark winter night, the icy wind moaning over its timbers, a train whistling in the distance as I frantically raced to get to the other side. I was terrified of being caught in the middle of the bridge with trains coming either way on the double tracks. There were little platforms at regular intervals along the span of the bridge where a person could stand and squeeze out of the way, but they hung out over the side of the bridge and I'd fought the sensation that I would pitch head long down into the chasm below.

The creek, which had seemed a river when I was a boy, trickled along its course the same as ever, meandering and twisting its tortuous way in the deep gully that had once seemed like a canyon. Its slopes were heavily wooded and I had spent much time there alone, hiding in the trees, making secret shelters, smoking cigarettes that I had found, dreaming of what my life might be like someday. Well now I knew how it had so far turned out. 'Still a chance to make good, old son, just change your attitude and maybe your luck will too. Go home and get on with it.' I plodded up the hill on the far side of the creek bank admonishing myself to quit talking to myself like some sort of motivational guru. I realized how weary I was and that my entire being was incapable of normal, rational function or thought. I hoped to have a good night's sleep without anymore of the silly recriminations that ricocheted inside my head.

I checked into the room I had reserved. Too tired to eat supper, I lay on the bed watching television, thinking of my father lying in his hospital bed only a few blocks away. For a few minutes I conspired again to go visit him, but could not bring myself to it. Again I was confounded by how to call on someone you had already said a final good bye to and realized that I did not have the resources for any more. Amusedly, I envisioned myself collapsing in a heap in the hospital and ending up in the bed next to my father. 'You're one sick puppy, only you could think of something like that,' I smiled to myself as the ludicrous image flashed in my mind.

Unfortunately, the Holiday Inn where I stayed was filled with families attending a baseball tournament and the halls echoed with noisy children and adults most of the night. I slept poorly and felt a total wreck by morning. Checking out I caught an express bus to the airport in Toronto. The driver talked of retirement with one of the other passengers and their conversation turned to speculations on what a great place British Columbia would be to settle. I remembered how I had envisioned British Columbia before I had first seen it, the promised land of eternal rain, rugged frontier mountain scenery in all directions. I was part of that scenery now, I thought. It was home. This place was just somewhere I had once passed through and I realized that I had little sense of longing for the area where I had grown up. 'Maybe it would seem better under other circumstances,' I thought, 'But I feel better already knowing that I'm leaving it behind again.'

At the airport I waited in a room with several other standby passengers. It was so crowded that I had to stand and I despaired of getting a seat on the daily flight to Vancouver. Twenty minutes after the flight was due to leave, I was assigned the last available seat and rushed across the terminal, boarding the aircraft at the last possible moment. I settled in my seat and closed my eyes, so very glad that the frantic week was behind me, feeling numb at the realization that I had said my final good-bye to my father and my old hometown. The noises of the aircraft preparing for the flight seemed to drift off and I faded into sleep before takeoff. I awoke momentarily as the jet raced down the runway, lifted its nose and left the ground. For a minute I watched the urban sprawl and writhing freeways beneath the tilting wing and then we rose into cloud and my view of the ground was gone. I slept. Later in the flight I awoke, went to the washroom and settled back in my seat and looked down on the prairie scenery far below. Suddenly on a reciprocal heading, another aircraft flashed by beneath, probably with a closing speed of over a thousand miles per hour. I thought, 'It never ends, the coming and going and I don't know which is which anymore.' I slept again and awoke shortly before the flight touched down in Vancouver. The rich colour of the scenery was startling and bathed in vivid emerald greens, dark umber, and the bright tones of new leaves emerging. The brilliant white of mountain peaks gleamed against the clear, deep blue sky of a perfect west coast spring afternoon. I had come home, my mission completed. For the moment, nothing else mattered.

Chapter 5

Mother

M.T. 'Bandera'

Allison Harbour, B.C.

Dear Mom:
May 31,1997

As usual I am writing from aboard a tugboat; at least this time, I'm using my computer so you can read my writing for a change. Also, as usual, I hope this finds you happy and well with lots to do and to look forward to. This is not an easy letter to write, because it is about dad.

I have had a very hectic month as I had to go to Oakville and put dad's affairs in order. I received a phone call from his doctor at the beginning of the month saying that dad had been in hospital for some time and that he had several serious health problems, including a brain tumour. I spent the first eight days of this month on the tug. During that time the specialists confirmed that the tumour was malignant and that he had only a few weeks to live. Dad has been living alone for the last few years. Suspecting that things might well be a mess, I flew to Oakville as soon as possible. I was there for seven days. I will spare you all the details; it was a very difficult time. However, I did manage to get power of attorney and got most things all organized. They were indeed a mess. It was a miserable ordeal, but I am happy that I was able to go and take care of things, it made Dad happy, and in the long run things will be a lot easier.

Dad was in and out of awareness of things but did not seem to be suffering, although he was doing a good job of making life a misery for the hospital staff. Fortunately his brother Henry and cousin Clarissa were able to come from England and spend a few days visiting and putting some old battles to rest, which seemed beneficial for every one. Of course, in the end we all had to leave him there and go about our lives. It doesn't seem right, but what else is there to do but get on with the business of living? I had some wonderful visits with dad during the times that he was lucid, recalling old memories and sorting out fact from fiction. I did my share of weeping, not for him (we all have to go some time), but rather for all that was lost, and all that should have been but never was. He had gone totally blind as the cancer progressed, which really frustrated him. However, he seemed at peace and said that he was ready to go. He indicated that he was proud of his children, and also that he deeply regretted not having sorted things out with you, and not coming to B.C. to live so long ago.

It is too late now for regrets or for anger. He felt that, while he would do a lot of things differently if he could, he has not had a bad life. I said my final good-bye two weeks ago today and left him with an armload of his beloved roses, which he seemed to enjoy very much. It is very hard to make final arrangements while someone is still alive, but it seemed the only way to do it in consideration of the circumstances. At least dad had the benefit of knowing that his eldest son was looking after things and that there was a family that still cared, despite all he has done to alienate us all.

It was mutually agreed between dad, myself, Ruth and Ryan (our other brother) that funerals are for the living. As Dad had few friends in Oakville, I have made all the arrangements, with his approval, for cremation. There was no will, a lot of bills, no estate, and very little money so we are not going to any unnecessary expenses. We will scatter his ashes here, probably on Newcastle Island, among the wild roses looking out to the mountains across the sea.

I am still sorting through the belongings that were worth shipping home to Nanaimo. I am finding many wonderful old photos from his childhood and early days in Canada. There are even some old memorabilia: his boat ticket and train ticket to Canada, his old suitcase, his old jewellery box and Bulova watch. I was too tired and busy and not in the mood for visiting, so I did not look anyone up. However it is twenty-six years since I left Oakville so, to stay sane, I did some travelling around. I got lots of photos of places we used to live in Oakville, Milton, Kilbride, etc. I was even in the barn on Lingren's farm on the Dundas highway! The farm is all gone (subdivisions and golf courses), but the barn was still standing and even smelled the same as it did when I was three years old! I also took a photo of the Zimmerman house, but no name was in the phone book so I did not call.

Braeside Camp is now twice as big as it was; Paris is exactly the same. The general store, water-trough and the house where we lived in in Kilbride are all still there as well! I also spent some time in the library doing research. I made several photocopies of pages from 1956 & 1957 Oakville newspapers (A&P Supermarket: Bread 15 cents a loaf !). If you are interested, I'd be happy to show them to you. Downtown Oakville is still very much the same as it was in the fifties, but north of town is now nearly all golf-courses, subdivisions and industrial areas.

Anyway: the reason that I am writing now is that my mind is fairly clear at the moment. I have been able to get a little rest out here thanks to some bad weather that forced us to tie the boat up. We have just managed to finally sell the condo, so on top of the book, the boat, and dad's business, we now have to find, buy and move to a new house. Everything is going to be a muddle for a while. Chances are that when dad's time comes, I'll probably be back out here on a tug boat. I am going to give Ruth this letter to mail to you when that time comes. She can add a note to tell you when he went.

The reason that we have kept the news from you is that there was nothing anyone could do for him and we did not want you to feel that we in any way expected you to do something. I felt that telling you by letter was kinder than slamming you with the news on the telephone. I hope I've done the right thing. Hopefully the next time we communicate, there will be some happier news.

Lots of love as ever
Fred

A little over a year after my sister, brother and I had scattered our father's ashes, mother came for a visit. I drove to the Victoria airport to meet her flight. I t had been over three years since my sister or I had seen her. The drive to her home in the Okanagan where she lived alone was only a few hours from Vancouver, but neither of us could bring ourselves to endure the misery of a visit with her. She was the unhappiest person that either of us knew.

Mother had always been that way. If anything were profitable, pleasurable or intellectual, it was evil. I called her the Angel of Gloom. She was a maniacal fundamentalist Christian, who chose to interpret her Bible in such a way that she could find little joy in life. It was her own interpretation of course, and she ended up drifting eternally from one church to another, always moving, spurred on by her contention that 'Everyone was out to get her' or that Satan was clearly among the congregation. She often proclaimed that she could not wait to escape 'this veil of tears', so that she could go to heaven where the streets were paved with gold and all was eternal bliss. She was only content when she had something to complain about, which she always did, or was certain that she was making someone else's life an utter hell.

I dreaded having anything to do with her, as did my sister. We each carried guilt about our feelings; we had endured more than enough at the woman's hand. Nevertheless hope springs eternal and I thought that perhaps this time things could be different. After all, she was our mother, and my sister and I both ached to have a normal relationship with her. We felt remorse that she was alone and lonely, but she had always made it impossible to get along. I ruminated in advance how best to deal with her, and counselled myself to be patient above all else. Despite her eccentricities, she was old and deserved some consideration. Ruth and I had reviewed with each other how to orchestrate a smooth visit. Going to meet her alone, I hoped, would give me an opportunity to ease into the visit, testing the waters, and to assess which mood and madness my mother was indulging in that particular day.

To my delight, the day was clear and warm. Mother was quite concerned about the damp coastal climate and how it affected her 'artheritis'. If it had been raining, or even cloudy, her complaining would begin before we left the airport. She was, on top of everything else, a consummate hypochondriac and had claimed more health problems than a flock of inbred sheep. In actual fact she was healthy as a workhorse, with enviable strength, little old lady that she was. Hopefully the flight would bring her in good condition and spirit, whisking her to us in less than two hours from the time she had locked her condominium door.

The alternative travel method was a four hour drive and a two hour ferry crossing, which would leave her exhausted and especially cranky. On her last visit, she claimed to feel seasick for two days after the ferry trip, even though the waters had been millpond smooth. So what could possibly be wrong today? I stood at the arrivals gate and waited to find out. All the other passengers had left by the time she finally appeared, pushing her wheeled 'walker', a heavy bag hanging from a strap around her neck. She was clinging to the arm of a young flight attendant and wearing her best sad abandoned puppy look.

Although the afternoon was warm, she wore a parka over a sweater. Winter boots rose almost to her knees. An old beach hat was pulled down over her ears and the large goggled glasses that she wore. After a cursory hello she wanted to know if I had 'got a pitcher of the plane?' When I said that I had not, she exclaimed, 'Darn it, I've always got a pitcher of the plane I flew on. I said to that stewardess that they should have postcards with pitchers of their planes and she said that was a good idea! I bought some new filum for my camra but I didn't put it in because I didn't have any tape to put around the edges in case the light leaked in and ruined the filum. I've had that problem before.'

Her walker was a wheeled contraption with hand brakes, a cargo basket and a padded seat. A wooden cane hung from one handle. 'It's my knees. They give out on the cement and I have to sit down.' There didn't seem to be much wrong with her knees at the moment, I observed, as she used the sturdy green cart to batter a path through the crowd standing by the baggage carousel. She sat on her walker and directed me in the retrieval of her bags. One was a huge green container with wheels and the other was a smaller bag with a huge padlock hanging from the zipper. I dragged them off the conveyor and wondered if they were full of tire irons. How had she managed them on her own?

On the way out to the parking lot she briskly wheeled her walker ahead of me and launched herself over the edge of a curb. The walker lurched forward and she followed on top of it, a heap of confused old lady staggering to keep her balance. I rescued her from careening in front of a taxi pulling away from the curb. We safely made our way the remaining distance to my small car and I began stowing mother and baggage. The dog had been waiting in the back seat. Usually quite gregarious, she chose to ignore mother, which I knew was a very bad sign. Whenever the dog did that, it was a certain that there was something especially malevolent about the person she was avoiding. Dogs know.

I helped mother into the front seat and tried to separate her from the two bags that she still clutched. There was not enough room for the bags. I finally persuaded her to part with one but not before she removed 'the stuff I might need', which included yet another coat, a bottle of water and a bag of sandwiches. 'It's no fun being old,' she droned, 'I'm seventy-one now you know, the same age as the queen!' 'Yes, mom, I know,' I said, musing that she had always enjoyed telling people she was the same age as the queen and that she'd been complaining about being old since she was in her forties.

I suggested that if she felt able, it would be a nice day to show her a little bit of Victoria before we began the drive north to Nanaimo. She had never been there before and I hoped that she would enjoy seeing something entirely new. Withdrawing a sandwich, she said that would be a good idea. Then she immediately began to complain about the condominium where she lived in the Okanagan. Before we had driven out of the airport parking lot she had launched herself into a litany of woes. 'If only I'd known what I was in for I would never have bought the place! Everybody there is a Jehovah's Witness, or a communist, or a Hell's Angel! They don't give you a moment's peace, always watching you and playing their loud music. They smear blood on the doors and have oral sex in the swimming pool. And the stink of some of the stuff they cook! Smells like the very pit of hell.' There was only one way of dealing with mother when she began to rave. Tune out and turn off! Most of the woes inflicted on her were imaginary and she simply wanted the satisfaction of having a captive audience. 'I just need somebody to listen to me.' It had nothing to do with senility; she had always been like that. 'Damn her!' I thought, 'Not into her visit ten minutes and it's begun already.'

Her condominium was a favourite theme. She had sold her house and bought the condo just as her second husband was dying of lung cancer. He was a derelict alcoholic she had met one day sitting on a park bench. Despite being paranoid of most people and the world around her, my mother indulged in random acts of benevolence, and had somehow reformed old Josh and persuaded him to marry her. I suspect that her main interest had been Josh's pension cheques. He was a war hero and drew a veteran's allowance as well as an old age pension. I remembered him as a kindly, quiet fellow, patient and gentle. Josh had a box full of medals he had earned during the world war two. Eventually he had snapped when he reviewed all the killing and destruction he had helped incur. He was a member of a military force as completely capable of rape, loot and pillage as the evil enemy. Guilt and horror possessed him, and Josh had spent most of his ensuing life as a skid row bum, a Lysol drinker and a general low-life. He was the essence of all that his mother abhorred. 'It had to be the damned pension cheques,' I mused. Mother had worked old Josh like an animal; he had suffered three hernia surgeries because of the heavy lifting and hard labour he had performed at her bidding.

She nagged and badgered him incessantly. I knew all too well what she was capable of, and understood when Josh finally hit her one day, knocking her cold. He spent a little time in jail because of that, and left the old woman soon after to live with my sister. Mother did not know where he was for over six months, and he enjoyed the sense of family that he had finally found. He returned to the old woman shortly before it was discovered that he was dying, which he had probably known already. I am convinced that Josh simply gave up, turning his face to the wall to escape the hopeless misery of life with the old hag. Mercifully he died quickly and quietly, a victim of huge injustice all his life.

Mother had been able to pay off the mortgage on her house, and then had sold it. She bought her condominium with the proceeds and now was terrorizing the other occupants of the building. I cringed to think of what it must be like having her for a neighbour. She had been railing on for years about the horrible place where she lived and I knew there was no point in trying to convince her that if she kept having the same problems everywhere she went - well! I had considered visiting her several times but could not bear the consequences of whatever she would try to embroil me in at her condominium.

She had a way of repelling a person and then leaving them feeling guilty for abandoning her, but to preserve temper and sanity there was no way anyone could stand being near her for long. Several of her brothers reside in the same town but some had lived there for years before she knew that they were nearby. Those who did visit her set themselves an agenda, so that they would have legitimate excuses to cut short their visits. She always complained that everyone is too busy to have any time for her. It was a sad situation, but one that only she could change and she seemed unable or unwilling to let a little joy into her life and the lives of those who wanted to love her.

Now as we drove into Victoria I took a scenic route and tried to show her various points of interest. I took her to where we could see Mount Baker and D'Arcy Island, a former leper colony. She babbled on incessantly about people and events of which I knew nothing. She seemed to take notice of nothing, her eyes downcast at some focal point on the dashboard. I pointed out several of the grand homes along Dallas Drive, an area that tour buses patrol because of the obvious opulence and spectacular architecture juxtaposed against some of the finest scenery on the continent. Her only comment was that she hoped I was 'not getting any big ideas'. I assumed she thought that I wanted to own one of these grand homes, but there was no point in trying to explain that I simply thought that she might have been interested in seeing them.

I explained about the Strait of Juan de Fuca, the international border, ships passing and the Olympic Mountains. I told her how, on bright sunny days, the mountains appeared to suddenly loom near and on dull days they receded into the distance. That inspired her to talk about grain elevators on the prairies, which in turn led her into a bleak monologue about one of her brothers. It was apparent to me that she was neither seeing nor appreciating any of her surroundings. People come from around the world, spending thousands to see this incredibly unique and beautiful area. Mother showed no interest. We stopped at Ogden Point ,where I tried to point out the long pier that protected the harbour mouth. There were several large naval vessels moored inside but, even though their massive grey hulls loomed over us, her monologue about things far away and long ago continued.

'Mom, it's almost rush hour, the traffic will be getting heavy. If you're not that interested in seeing Victoria, we can go straight home.'
'Fred,' she replied guardedly, 'I just need somebody to talk to. I don't have anybody to listen to me, I just need to talk.'
'Yes mom, I understand, you can talk about whatever you want all the way to Nanaimo. There's no point in fighting traffic downtown and looking for parking spots if you just need somebody to talk to. I can't show you anything if you won't pay attention.'
'Fred, I am interested, but why won't anybody let me talk?' she screeched.
'Look mom, right now you're in Victoria. Look at all the

people on the streets. Most of them have come a long way. See, there's a busload from Japan. Forget about life on the homestead sixty years ago and what's wrong with everything where you live now. You are here now, that is all that matters. There is no point in being here if you'd rather be somewhere else.' I was furious with her, my voice rising as I spoke. 'I'm just wasting your time and my time by doing this. I'd hoped we could have a good time and that you could see something different, but there's no point if you're going to carry on like this!' Her face took on the special look she reserved for a tantrum and suddenly I realized that I had pushed her too far.

Clamping her hands over her ears as we drove by the provincial legislature buildings, she began to screech, 'Shut up, Satan, shut up, Satan. In the name of Jesus, shut up, Satan. That's not you speaking, son, that's Satan. I recognize you everywhere, Lucifer! In the name of Jesus be gone!'
'Mom, no, it's me Fred, your son. Now stop this nonsense. We don't need to begin your visit like this. Please stop, right now!' 'Shut up Satan, shut up Satan, shut up Satan!' with her hands over her ears, she repeated her mad edict over and over. She was loud enough to attract attention from the tourists on the sidewalks.

Seething, embarrassed, fighting an urge to hit her, I tried to concentrate on manoeuvring in the traffic. The tirade continued all the way out of the city and along the highway. She kept her hands over her ears, muttering gibberish, apparently trying to impress me that she was deep in prayer. Any time that I tried to speak she would begin to screech again 'Shut up Satan, shut up Satan'. Intermittently she would wave her arms furiously and twice grabbed at the steering wheel. I seized her arm and held it down, amazed at the incredible strength she possessed. 'Look mom,' I roared, 'Stop your bullshit right now! That is enough! If you want to get to heaven in a hurry, do it on your time! We're going to have a head-on collision if you keep this up, now settle down.' I waved my cellular phone at her. 'Anymore of this foolishness and I'm calling 911 for an ambulance to meet us. They can give you a shot in the ass and pack you off to the hospital.' She was suddenly placid and subdued. 'Son,' she said quietly, 'You're going to heaven whether you like it or not. I've seen to that. You don't have any choice in what God has planned for your life.'

I had not regained control of my anger and was unable to employ the restraint that would have kept her calm. 'How dare you presume to speak for God? All your life you conveniently pass the buck on your God, or Satan, as it suits you. You never accept responsibility for yourself. Now if this is how your visit is going to go I may as well take you back to the airport right now. I'm not bringing you home to my house if this is how you intend to perform. I'm sure you don't want to stay in Satan's house anyway. Ruth has too many other problems to deal with so I'm not sure I want to take you to her home either if you can't act like a mother coming to visit her family. We've really looked forward to you coming and have planned and planned how to make sure you have a nice time, but you're ruining everything already.' 'You've always been like this,' she roared at me and burst into tears. 'Always demanding attention and trying to run the show. Ever since you were two years old, you wanted to be the boss!'
'Attention? I bloody well got it, didn't I? At least one beating a day as far back as I can remember,' I shot back at her.
'Well you kept asking for it!'
'Oh shit, listen to yourself. How can you admit to beating your children and justify it at the same time? Spare the rod and spoil the child? I guess it didn't work did it?'
'Shut up Satan, shut up Satan!'
'Mom, we have another hour until we get to Ruth's house. I'm not going to say another thing. You've got until then to decide how you want things. Dad is gone. We don't know how much longer any of us have. Who knows? You may bury me.

Today is the only day that we've got. We have to make the best of it. If nothing is going to change and this is the way we're going to get along then there's no point. I can't handle it. It's better if we have nothing to do with each other. So if you intend to keep it up, have a good look. This is your flesh and blood that you are seeing for the last time. I am forty-six years old. This bullshit has gone on my whole life and I have had enough!'

'Shut up Satan!'

I telephoned ahead to my sister to advise her that mother wouldn't be staying at Satan's house and that I was bringing mother around to her place instead, if that were possible. When we finally arrived, there were children running all over and I could not get Ruth aside to brief her on the events of the afternoon. Mother was still in the car, lying across the seats with her hands over her ears shouting, 'Shut up Satan, shut up Satan.' Ruth had the picture immediately.

The visit wore on. Ruth's house was small by contemporary standards. It was brimming with children of all ages and there was only one tiny bathroom. Ruth moved the two youngest children into her bedroom and let mother stay there, next to the bathroom. Mother divided her time between the two rooms. She would spend hours in the bathroom, oblivious to the needs of the rest of the household. Then she would spend more hours closed in her room, holding loud, angry dissertations with herself behind the door. I had bruised her arm when I had restrained her during the drive home. Usually she wore sweaters with the sleeves turned down, but now she rolled them up so that everyone could see what Satan had done to her.

She spent time with the youngest children, playing tirelessly. Ruth observed that mother seemed best able to relate to the infants; they were probably on a level closest to her own. She had to be watched closely because she would suddenly launch into tirades at the youngsters and could instantly terrify them. I telephoned regularly to monitor how everything was going. I felt guilty that, with only my wife and I living in a much larger house with two bathrooms, mother was staying at my sister's crowded house. Several days passed before Ruth felt that it was probably safe to risk bringing her around to my place for a visit. My brother-in-law came along, just in case, and the visit went well. It seemed that mother was always able to act rationally when she was in the company of several people. It was when she was alone with someone that she was most likely to begin her absurd performances.

One lovely late summer day everyone went for a picnic with mother at a local beach. The day passed smoothly and she had a good time. Braced for every possibility, we did not. In the late afternoon Ruth and I took her to the place where our father's ashes were scattered. We were prepared for an outburst but she endured the occasion placidly, softly murmuring, 'Rest in peace, old boy.' She sighed and exclaimed, 'I always knew he had a brain tumour!' Then she turned her attention to the splendour of the day. Ruth and I had thought that visiting this place would be the focus of her entire week. We had been dreading it, but all seemed to pass quietly.

I was going to sea in two days. Ruth and I decided that things were going so smoothly that it would be best I say goodbye to mother while she was in a positive mood. We had spent the week on tenterhooks. Hopefully there would be no more tantrums during her visit. 'Perhaps she's blown her wad,' I said, musing that she had worked the poison out of her system the first day. I was, however, unwilling to take the risk of inadvertently provoking her again. She mumbled an apology for how things had gone that day, suggesting that perhaps we had both been over tired. I accepted that but made no promises I could not keep. There was no way I intended to visit her at her home.

Mother spent the next two days preparing for her return trip. She always made a huge issue out of the most mundane things and devoted a large portion of her visit to fussing over nothing. 'At least it kept her occupied and out of the way,' Ruth conceded, as she mentioned how mother remained closeted in her room but was now singing and laughing to herself, apparently enjoying a major mood shift. She was leaving. The past week had seemed an eternity. Everyone was exhausted and relieved the ordeal was ending, yet guilty for feeling that way. Mother had once again launched a campaign about coming to live in a local nursing home and had pointedly remarked that her 'arthritis' didn't seem to bother her anymore. She was, of course, implying that a move to Nanaimo was now within her consideration.

Both Ruth and I recoiled at the idea of mother living in the same town as us. We bore tremendous guilt about feeling that way about our mother, but we both knew that there was no way to achieve a workable situation with her. There was no way of pleasing her. Ruth recalled how our grandmother, mother's mother, had become an outrageous problem while in a nursing home during her last years. The frail, blind, old woman had once ripped a bathtub loose from its fastenings during a fit of anger. She became so violently upset whenever any of her children visited, that the nursing home pleaded with them to stay away. The old lady had spent the last year of her life entirely alienated from her own children and had died of pneumonia, all alone.

My sister and several of her children drove mother back to the airport in Victoria. I had implored Ruth not to take her alone and to make sure that she sat as far away from the steering wheel as possible. We both recalled that reaching for the steering wheel was an old habit of hers, something she had often done while our father had been driving. All went well, however, and mother phoned Ruth to say that she had arrived home safely. It would probably take her another week to unpack and recover from her trip.

A few days later severe weather hit the coast with hurricane force winds in some places. Newscasts were filled with speculation about the early onset of winter storms. Mother telephoned my wife to inquire about my safety at sea, a pointed attempt to show an interest, her way of expressing sincere regret for the unhappy visit. After all the wasted years, it was a start. Perhaps there is a chance for a happy ending. In my heart, I believed that nothing was going to change at this point in my mother's life. 'But,' I thought to myself, 'Shut up Satan.' I was wrong. There was hope.

Mom returned home to her condominium, a complex for seniors in the heart of the Okanogan. When she had first left my father and moved west, mom and my sister lived on the goodwill of immediate family and acquaintances from local churches. She worked at housekeeping and in the orchards, all the while living an incredibly frugal existence as she, 'scrimped and saved.'

Eventually, combining her resources with a brother, the two bought a small parcel of land and each erected their own tarpaper shacks on opposite corners of the property. Neither had even enough basic schooling to be fully literate, and each had inherited similar aberrant personalities. My mother, the eternal hypochondriac who so often claimed to be ill, had survived by relying on my sister Ruth to do a major amount of the household chores, including carrying water and firewood until late into the evenings. Then she attended to her schoolwork. Anyone else mother could coerce into helping with her ongoing building program would soon be pressed into service. Despite her meagre earnings and pitiable income from social assistance, mother eventually converted her rural holding into a small house in town. After finishing high school, my sister was finally able to escape mother's sinister grasp, albeit to a parallel fate. Mother found herself a second husband in old Josh. Together they worked and renovated the little house until old Jim succumbed to cancer. Mother sold the house and bought the condominium unit. It was a remarkable accomplishment for someone who had started out with grade three schooling and a faltering grasp on how the world worked.

Sadly, living alone soon recalled all her demons and mother descended again into madness. She complained incessantly about the other residents. They were all, 'Satanists, Jehovah's Witnesses, or Hell's Angels.' In the heat of the Okanogan summer, she would often sit in a folding chair in the underground parking area until the cooler early hours of the morning, a startling apparition to other residents returning home. One winter she decided that a draught was coming from a baseboard heater. She retired to bed after cramming the heater with a wool blanket, and awoke to find a fireman standing in her bedroom. He was there in response to the smoke alarm she had triggered. She was incensed about 'the pervert in a rubber coat' who had invaded her privacy.

She developed contempt for a neighbour in the unit beneath hers, an ailing elderly lady who was being cared for by her son. Mother went so far as writing a letter to the 'Atterny Genral' (sic) about the 'insecent marigwana smok' (sic). As her campaign for clean air escalated, she began hurling pickle jars filled with water from her second floor balcony. My sister received a telephone call from the local health care unit. They persuaded mother that she would be safe from the smoke and intimidating neighbours if she came peaceably. Incarcerated in the local hospital, she was safe from herself and in turn, the world was safe from her.

Fortuitously, she was placed in a geriatric psychiatric facility where she would remain for the last three years of her life. The attention she received was kind and loving. She thrived, despite knee-replacement surgery and the discovery of terminal cancer. To the family's amazement she began to demonstrate compassion for fellow residents, and found pleasure in the simple kindnesses we were able to offer her. For the first time, we her children were able to love her without reserve or trepidation.

Mother, the lifelong fundamentalist zealot, who had so long wanted to 'cross the Jordan and be with Jesus', finally found her toes wet in the edge of the river. The doctor had given her six months; she fought death for the next two years. I visited her very near the end, stunned to find a near-skeletal shell of the woman who had been my eternal nemesis. She was sleeping. I sat beside her and rested. Finally she awoke briefly and clearly recognized me. She took my hand in hers, now bent and gnarled with arthritis. Her eyes had become a clear blue, as mine are. Looking into them she whispered, 'Thank you,' then fell asleep again. It was the last she spoke to either of her children . That one word expressed the gratitude and love which I had so long sought from her. It brought an acceptable end to life-long fractiousness and pain-filled relationships. She died peacefully in her sleep a few days later while my sister sat beside her.

It was all over. Now - they were both gone.

A Son's Eulogy to His Mother

December 31, 2003

Thank you all for coming here so early on a snowy holiday morning to say goodbye to my mother, Hazel Stuart. We are gathered here as brothers and sisters, as a family, as dear friends, as her daughter, and I her son.

Mom died slowly, but gracefully and placidly through the past months. She faded away in recent weeks and finally her body stopped quietly while sleeping on Sunday morning. I suppose we could say that she left a little early for church that day. Her daughter, my sister, was by her side and I choose to believe it was that presence which gave Mom the release to leave this life and its trials behind.

We had all been blessed with plenty of time to say thank you, goodbye and I'm sorry. She passed away with closure, both for herself and all of us. Now this morning I stand here groping for words. Those of you who know me understand that for me this is most unusual, and I apologize for reading my thoughts but I am sure you understand.

It is difficult to eulogize the person who gave me life and then stood as the largest enigma in my existence, and also for many others here today. I am not given to flowery words and I have known death often. I understand its place in the cycle of being for all living things. Yet today it is my mother's death I must deal with, the eldest child who now moves next in line toward my own inevitable passing. So I am indeed at a bit of a loss for words. I cannot eulogize my mother with facetious accolades. I cannot glorify a life that was often deeply troubled. By all accounts she struggled with an illness for nearly her whole life that constantly betrayed her and alienated her from those who would love her. All too often her life, in her own words was, 'a veil of tears.'

However, I doubt that few of us would be here today if she had let that affliction rule over her to the end. Thanks in part to modern medical science, but also to mom's own spirited determination, she achieved what many do not. In the end she was able to receive and reciprocate love freely. Mother gloried in each day and held an enthusiasm for life that amazed and delighted all of us. She fought death with a quiet stoicism and never turned her face to the wall. She kept her dignity to the end. Look around you here. Everyone came today to remember her for her grace, her kindness, and her warmth. What a triumph!

Funerals are not for the dead but rather for those of us who go on living. Today let us celebrate life, not mourn for the finiteness of our passing as a brief moment within the infinite history of the universe. In the words of the writer John Berger: 'Whisper not for that which has been lost. Not out of nostalgia, but because it is on the site of loss that hope is born.' May we go forward into the balance of our lives reaffirming that dreams __ARE__ possible to achieve. With all the base and all the grand things that define humanness, perhaps hope is the greatest. My mother, Hazel Stuart, will live on not only through her children and her family, but also with the inspiration of her final courage.

A description of life, refined to purest eloquence, is composed of three elements:

- Someone to love, something to do, something to look forward to.

Truly Hazel Stuart, our friend, our sister, our mother, our grandmother, when her course was finished, lived a full and wonderful life.

And Now They Are Both Gone

Despite the relief of the end of her suffering and the sudden lifting of the dark cloud of her existence, I can still find no peace. There is an awareness of being next in line to the grave, and I often feel that death will be a release from the weight of my existence. Perhaps, if there another life, and as I learn more I believe that there is, I will be able to advance to a higher self, where I will live with confidence, trust, a positive energy and a sense of good purpose. Perhaps this existence is a preparation for something that lies ahead in a future I cannot comprehend. Certainly I find a peculiar sense of closure in knowing that I have no children to whom I can pass on the genetic madness which has apparently descended through the last visible generation of my family.

As a stepfather I was and am a failure. Despite my clear awareness of what not to do, I often found myself sitting on my shoulder watching in horror as I began to do the same things my parents had done to me. I can never describe the pain and loneliness of those times of being out of control. Yet I was able to recognize that my instincts, be they products of nurture or nature, were wrong and I sought help. My parents could have done the same thing. Or could they have?

That is yet another question which will remain forever unanswered. As the years advance and I continue to grapple with the dilemma of my existence, I have tried to convince myself that, despite the wrongness of their ways, both my parents did their best. So often my father declared that, 'If it was good enough for me, then it is good enough for you.' I still curdle at the unjustness and blindness of that concept. That cavalier dismissal is merely another way of avoiding personal responsibility. In all things, a great motivation for me is to consider the effect of my words and actions on the lives of others, especially the young and vulnerable. I hasten to suggest that we are all responsible for others' lives. In accepting that, and in acting responsibly, we enrich our own lives.

I grope for a succinct and dramatic conclusion to this narrative. I know it is an account of a life that is merely another grain of sand on the shores of human history. This story is, at best, a mile's walk in someone else's shoes. Sadly I know that those shoes fit many others' feet. In an age described by many as 'The Information Revolution', many are convinced that there are more perverse and aberrant individuals than ever before. I disagree. We are merely more aware of social injustice and human misery than ever before. With that increased awareness, do we react more vigorously to right the wrongs we choose to perceive? We export billions in offshore aid and weakly affect one disaster while ignoring all the others, often just as dramatic and tragic. While we assuage our conscience with token acts of distant kindness, there are so many within the cast of our glance whose pain is as real as any other victim. If only we would each attend the problems in our own yard, what a wonderful world we could have!

Epilogue

The following candid pages are offered as a final insight. These pages are painfully intimate and I have included them in this book with no small trepidation. However, if someone who has never personally known the depths of clinical depression can understand that the disorder is an uncontrollable force and not an exercise in self-pity, then my effort has been a success. If someone who endures the manic depths of darkness can understand that they are not alone in their despair, my work is a success. It is worth mentioning that many, if not most, of the world's most brilliant people permanently suffer from this disorder. People are shocked to learn some of the names of those who can be diagnosed as manic depressive. Famous composers, scientists, painters, writers, statesmen - so many seem to possess this darkness that balances on a thin line in counter to their particular brilliance. Hence the term: bi-polar disorder. If you are cursed to find yourself afflicted with this particular illness, try to see your place among your peers. Focus on the bright side of the equation.

Saying Goodbye

Two weeks have passed since I learned that my father was in hospital, critically ill with a malignant brain tumour. A few days after receiving that information, I was called to duty at sea and so here I sit on a tugboat. Since sailing, I have learned that his condition is terminal; at best a few weeks remain for him. It is 03:00am on a Saturday morning and I am weary. Sleep is always difficult out here. Now this! There are arrangements to make, travel plans to organize, a brother and sister to consult. It is very challenging to do all that with a mobile phone from the B.C. north coast 'jungle'. At least a few days remain before I can get ashore and properly attend to the affairs at hand, if our weather begins to co-operate. In the meantime, my wife who is already very busy provides splendid support.

It is often said that one cannot steer a straight and accurate course by staring back at the wake behind the boat. Yet it seems I am required to do exactly that for the next while and my helmsman ship may be severely tested. It has been a long and tortuous journey, this relationship with my father. Those who know him, including his doctor, my sister and brother, all agree that he has always behaved in a bizarre fashion and even, at times, has been possessed by obvious madness. Despite his frailties and cruelties, his wilful alienation from his children, and his unpredictable tangents, he is still our father. Not that that is any sort of achievement. Having one sperm among millions find its way to the egg is not a conscious endeavour. As common an event for a mouse or a housefly, no-one should receive a personal accolade for the mechanics of universal biology. Yet, there is more than that. I cannot deny that I knew he was about to leave this life long before I received the word. There were premonitions, weird dreams about him. I was even prompted to write a letter to his second ex-wife asking her to contact me if this very sort of situation arose. Only a few months later, the call has come. How did I receive that signal from thousands of miles away? Clearly there is more to it than sperm and egg, nucleic acid and dividing cells.

Admittedly my ruminations on this subject are entirely selfish. I am concerned about the outcome of events because of how they will affect me. My father's tragic scenario is now in dénouement and the ending is entirely predictable. His misery is about to end. Ours may well continue, but that is up to us. In fact, after the endless cruelties and embarrassments endured at his hand, there is part of me that wants to go and press a pillow over his face as an act of mercy to end his suffering and vindicate mine. I should certainly feel no obligation to him after his eternal malevolence, and just for once I would be exercising some control over our tangential relationship. There are no terms of endearment, only a mild sense of guilt about feeling nothing. This is family. I feel an obligation to my brother and sister to tie loose ends. I function from a sense of duty rather than caring.

How I wish that I had had a father for whom I could grieve, a man who had reciprocated love with his children. The old prick! He has raped every one of his children, either in body or in mind, leaving us all, to varying degrees, filled with insecurities, paranoia, a sense of shame, and confusion about how to cope with the world around us. Clearly he did not know, so how could he have taught us? The only thing of value that has come to us is the strength which comes from eternal struggle. We his children have all had to be survivors of his grim doings. Our common bond is our dark legacy and how we each struggle to overcome it. It is time we did some living, just for the joy of it! Ding, dong, the old bastard is dying! The only reason we have to bury him is so that we can dance on his grave and then wash the dust from our feet.

Like being caught in a surreal art film, nothing makes sense. There is a vague sense of expectancy that perhaps the whole sordid affair will redeem itself and I am caught, mesmerized, waiting to see what happens next. Poetic justice says that, because he wishes his ashes spread on roses, I should instead concede the body to a dung heap and let the scavengers have their fill. At least feeding the creatures of the air and the worms of the earth would be one final positive act. As the ravens tear at his putrid flesh, croaking and hopping about, hopefully some remnant of his dark soul would remain to feel their prodding, ripping beaks and the humiliation of such cavalier abandonment. This would be a fitting reward for the ungrateful fool that he has worked so diligently to be. T he fading, closing shot could be a splatter of bird shit splashing into the ocean and dissolving into the abyss.

Obviously, malevolence is a hereditary trait. I feel vindictive. Perhaps it is a cloak to protect me from the coldness of my frustration. The anger that has been there so often was all I had to sustain me. I feel it yet. He is still alive in body as I write, but there is little I can do to bridge the gap without his participation. It seems pointless now to hope to gain his approval and pride of me and his other children and what we have accomplished. Vicariously, through us, his life has meaning and success despite the impediments he forced upon us. If only I could get him to understand that. The residue of his sordid existence need not repeat itself to produce yet another generation of wasted lives. We will rise above our genes; we will not live in futility.

Hopefully I can go to him before the dividing cells in his tortured brain consume the final circuits that sustain bodily function. I am prepared to deal with his ravings. Perhaps he will not even recognize me, his eldest son. He lies there waiting, drooling, shitting himself, babbling nonsense. It is not for his solace that I go, but mine. I am a man. I am used to death. I have heard it whisper in my own ear at times.

Someday, I know, I too will cease to exist. That day could be this one; this very heartbeat could be my last. It is not the dying that saddens me - we are all frail, inevitably mortal, as are even mountains and forests which are so much more than we are. Rather it is the wasted life, the lost laughter, the spurned love, the deliberate meaninglessness, the absence of dignity.

This is the purpose of attending the deathbed - dignity. I must be able to go and say to him that I accept his frailty, and that I forgive him as completely as I can, not for his solace, but mine. If I am man enough to find compassion for the one person who has hurt me most, and can show him that, then I achieve the strength to get on with what remains of my days and make the world a better place. Per ardua ad astra: through adversity to the stars. It is finished. It is a new beginning.

Sins of Our Fathers

He lies dying on the other side of the country
even as I sit here writing, far away in the night
on a storm-tossed sea where he does not know I am.

Manifestly he has no remorse even now
for all the pain inflicted on so many,
he can only mutter with feeble faltering breath
about the things he has never done
that are his sole regrets.

I try to stir a pleasant recollection from a dark, twisted past
but end up foundering yet again
through the anger, the misery, the violence
I can still see the raised thick-fingered fists
feel their stunning shattering, almost daily blows
as he tells me this hurts him more than me
'Spare the rod and spoil the child'.

For some reason the only good memory I can withdraw
is one day that he took me fishing
and how later we fried and ate the tiny, muddy bass
not knowing then those few magic hours
would have to last a lifetime.

The cold stark hurt of being cast out while still too young to
fly
on crippled mutant wings, without comprehension
after all the despairs already known at a tender age
even his failed marriage became my blame
and one excuse was as good as another
when I was just of nuisance value,
bastard spawn, 'If thine eye offend thee, pluck it out'.
A living hell, denied my childhood and then my only home.

Sins of the Fathers

Barely grasping only now, still not quite believing
that it was the very best he could do
immersed in his own inner agonies
staring into vacant distances, gnawing at his fingers until they
bled
trapped in never ending nightmares
enemy bombs whistling down, some exploding, some not
still hearing more approaching Luftwaffe engines
throbbing in the night sky above his English farmhouse
screaming gut-shot horses,
sudden dead silent teenage peers
spurned love
dead-end dreams
false hopes
convoluted scriptures, beatings
his own manic corporal religious father
perverse eternal haunting horrors
he did not have the strength to will away.

After so many fumbled wasted years
too young and ignorant and lost
to understand the blind pain I carried and passed on
like some infectious disease to those who tried to care
I am much older now and yet the only love I can offer to him
is a flickering resolve to try not to hate
but I cannot lose the hopeless sense
the bitter betrayal of never being able to please
his invented excuses to alienate his very flesh, his essence, his
son.

My triumphs, my struggles, my fears he never knew or
appeared to care
that all I wanted was to do him proud, just for once to have
approval
and it is not the pain nor dread that is the most heinous crime
but the wasted time, the buried talents, the unrequited lives.

Now his days are nearly done
one dark eternal second ticking slowly into another
all is lost and, closer ever closer
faceless screaming demons reach for him
their fetid breath felt stronger now
than that of those which have pursued him all lifelong,
he lies bitter and alone, afraid,
face to the wall he has built
just wanting to be left for once in peace.
Guiltily, part of me wants him to suffer, 'An eye for an eye'.

But he too was betrayed by his own father
now long dead but waiting still behind one more darkened
door
wildly driven also by some grievous, writhing burden
bestowed by yet another heavy-handed, black-souled father's
son
accursed inheritance, the infernal wheels keep turning
and the best that I can do
terrified that I am yet another demon son
is to acknowledge the dark facts
and thank the gods
that I have not replanted the spoiled and angry seed.

Sonless I often grieve
for what could have been, should have been, could yet be
but that is only false hope, no-one changes much alone
and I wonder if it's guilt or love that draws me to his deathbed
now
after more than thirty years away to try and somehow explain
that I understand his frailty, want to forgive his weakness
for beshitting himself for being just a man
offer him a last chance to voice affection, just once
afford him the solace of giving benediction
so that perhaps I can let it go
resigned to know when my time comes
that dark god-cursed circle

of the sins of the sons of the fathers is broken
there will be no more progeny
cursed with tortured souls.

Now Then

Now then, it is finished. Thank the gods. I am bloody weary of writing about all this damnable dying business. Wincing with the pain of fresh-broken ribs, I heaved the mooring lines ashore from the tugboat that I had been aboard for the past two weeks, and then telephoned home to say that I was on my way. I had waited on the news for weeks, but still it surprised me. The message had arrived only minutes earlier. He was dead, on his seventy-third birthday. He had slipped into a coma and stopped breathing from complications with pneumonia. It is, apparently, a common way to die of a brain tumour.

Arrangements had previously been made for dealing with the body and my brother and sister were notified. It was a relief that things were finally drawing to a conclusion. There was the wait for his remains and copies of the death certificate. Creditors had to be notified that they were out of luck. 'Your account with this man has been terminated.' There is a quiet, smug pleasure in telling them that. Silly, greedy bastards! They should have known better than to extend credit to the old wag. He never could manage money. All that remained to do was to contact his pension administrators, the tax department and writing DECEASED on any mail that came for him. It is over.

We no longer have to worry about what preposterous stunt he may next pull, nor about his incongruous claims and allegations. He was paranoid, psychotic, psychopathic, schizophrenic, and hypochondriac; an absolute emotional mess. At times he could display gems of genius and compassion toward strangers who did not know him yet, but he ended his life bitter and alone, even when he was with someone else. I am my father's son, and how I have struggled to overcome the stigma of his influence. Only now at middle age am I emerging from beneath the cloud of self-doubt and insecurity that I have allowed to fetter me all my life. He no longer haunts me. It does not matter if I could never please him, make him aware and proud, because now he is dead. I am alive, free at last.

His story could be entitled: 'The Postman Who Got Lost in the Mail', because that is exactly what happened. He had delivered mail for many years and one of his regular calls had been to a funeral home. He had befriended the mortician and wanted his remains to be dealt with there. His ashes were shipped but we waited and waited. The package had been lost 'somewhere in Manitoba - on a truck', they thought, although they also claimed he had been shipped by air. It was a holiday weekend and hopefully he would arrive 'sometime near the end of next week'. As was typical of his behaviour in life, he suddenly and surreptitiously appeared the next day in a white cardboard box, dropped on the sidewalk in my garden by a courier. Now things were winding down, I had the ashes in my grasp, literally. I sat with the awesome weight of that small box in my lap, and finally, after all the machinations of the ordeal, I wept. Five minutes later, my eyes clearing and my face drying, I was able to put him away and get on with my day. I put him in the cupboard with the rose fertilizer and the aphid powder. He loved gardening.

Five weeks after he died, we were able to put him to rest as he had asked. My sister, one of her sons and my brother rose before dawn and we travelled to a local waterfront park. As a blood-red sun rose beneath a grey, clouded sky, we uncapped the urn and set him free. I didn't tell them then that all of his ashes would not fit into the urn, which I had bought at a discount store. I flushed the rest down the toilet. Yes, it was a vindictive act, but it felt good.

There was a sultry, anxious feel to the day, even at daybreak. For the next week we were to have unseasonable, miserably stormy weather. They thought it was El Nino, but I tell you, it was my dad. No-one could think of much to say, save for a raven that anxiously hopped about in a nearby oak tree, croaking pathetically. We stood there for a few awkward minutes in silence and finally walked out on the beach to watch the imposing sunrise. Later we gathered briefly over a cup of tea and listened to a recording of Mantovani's 'Charmaine'. It seemed a fitting thing to do. This was the tune that I had heard on the car radio as I drove out of the old hometown after saying the last good-bye to dad while he was still alive. Eventually someone had to go, and soon we were all immersed again in our separate lives.

The place where we scattered Dad's ashes is in a waterfront public park. It is a beautiful place, often filled with happy relaxed people, playing children and friendly dogs. I take my dog there regularly. There is a broad, open, south-facing beach on one side and a large, drying salt-water lagoon on the other. Between the two, a path makes its way out to a rocky promontory and a small island covered in fir and oak trees. The view is splendid in all directions. On a clear day, you can see the coastal mountains across Georgia Strait, and sometimes even the buildings in Vancouver, almost forty miles away. Especially fine days allow distant Mount Baker, a dormant volcano, to loom above the entire panorama.

Along the path, above the driftwood, sedges and beach grasses grow. Low, wind- stunted arbutus and Garry oak trees are surrounded by thickets of blackberries, broom and wild roses. It is especially lovely in spring when they bloom. Sometimes in early morning, seals sun themselves on the beach. Occasionally, we have seen racoons there and even deer. They leave their tracks in the sand. There is always an abundance of birds. It is a place to celebrate life. He never came to visit us on Vancouver Island although he talked of it often and we always dreaded him coming. We never knew how to deal with him. Yet now he is gone, there will always be regret that he did not get to see this place at least once. Dad would have loved it here.

Ashes

For the first time in my life
I have my father absolutely in my control
his ashes are locked up in the garage
in a cabinet next to the rose fertilizer and aphid powder.
He loved gardening.

Until my brother and sister can join me
to scatter him on the wild roses by the sea,
cry a little, and then get on with our individual lives
he can stay there in a nondescript cardboard box
like so many chimney scrapings.

I have damned his eyes
for all the cruelty and ignorance
his wasted life, and mine,
but the postman brought the parcel today
and when I sat alone with five pounds of inert carbon
in a flimsy cardboard box,
all that remains of him
and my origins,
I couldn't help but weep.

Enough of this, he never shed a tear for me
and so I rise and bend to my chores
hoeing and weeding, tending the garden
I see my workman's hands, my crooked feet
the way I roll my socks down to my boots
my old khaki shorts and paint-stained shirt,
I catch myself pausing to watch a small bird in the hedge
and suddenly realize how much of him
lives on in me
despite all that I have done
to put those twisted roots behind me.

Sins of the Fathers

Time passed, we spread his ashes
in a place I often go to walk the dog
it's lovely there
in fair weather and in winter storms
each spring the wild roses bloom beneath a gnarled oak
beside the path
where couples stroll, children play, dogs stop to crap
life goes on without a pause in a stream of fleeting moments
that are each nothing of significance
but each time I pass there
I say hello to Dad and imagine
how he would have liked this place
and I am glad that this is where
we spread his ashes.

Rise up

Rise up
the day is come
my sister, my brother,
when we must go down on the seashore at first light
and spread our father's ashes
on the wild roses as we had promised him
before the tumult of the day
and the inquiring eyes of others
who cannot know for whom or how we grieve
for that which was never realized
and how we are cheated of our birthright
but at this late moment
yet hope to find our dignity.

Rise up
glimmering dawn
you blood red angry sun
harbinger of storm and gloom
shine down on these dew-laden roses
as we scatter the carboned remnants
crushed bones and ash
sifting through our fingers
charcoal of our essence
all that remains of he who was our father
and life-long cursed himself for being just a man.

Rise up
you bastard black raven
this is our spectacle alone
there is nothing here to eat
you defile our ritual
with your incessant croaking
hopping helter skelter
from branch to branch

mocking our simple need
to find meaning in our deed.
Or is that a benediction that you chant,
are you the manifestation
of some tormented spirit
come to claim this dust now as your kin?
He loved birds
so take this debris then
we leave you to it
eat it up if you will
then shit it out
we commit these bitter leavings to your realm
of tormented spirits and twisted legends
we do not care now
our task is done.

Rise up
foul wind
storm wrack
foaming spume
sing your mad-mouthed chant
of doom and sorrow
cast your bitter brine over
these thorny flowers
your breath stirs the last grey atoms
among the roots and branches
and your pelting wet missiles
drive our father's powdered remnants
down into the loaming darkness
of the ground.
For seven days and nights
your blasts continue
as if to erase all traces, to obliterate
the very memory of this mortal
whom we have consigned to the forces
of the revolving planet
and the whimsies of a world gone mad.

Fred Bailey

Rise up
you dancing kite
over this spring beach
kissed by laughing waters
silver sands sparkling
beneath leafy oaks
surrounded by fragrant flowering pink, wild roses.
The cries of mating birds
mingle with chatterings of happy children
who chase along before the promise of the day
a bounding puppy and a big red ball.
Strolling lovers, old and young
in this day of promise embrace
the hope of springs eternal
fresh and restless on our sacred shore.

Rise up
our shattered spirits
we may not be so fortuned
to be laid to rest in such a place.
If still we regret that which was not,
or rue the pain and ignorance of a wasted life
we have a full and ripe potential
to vindicate the tragic story
and provide good meaning
to this ending which becomes a beginning
for another story that shall make sense
from the sorrows that brought us to this place.

Drowning

He knew he should not be there; it was the worst place in the world for him to be, but he felt he had no choice in the matter. That pissed him off more than anything; the lack of choice, the lack of control. It seemed that everything about his life was controlled or affected by the influence or the presence of someone or something else. The easiest thing for him to do, he felt, was to rise out of his bunk and simply take the few steps outside to the bulwarks and throw himself overboard. But there were even choices beyond the act of jumping. What would it feel like, hitting that ice-cold water? Would he suddenly be filled with regret for his imminent death? Would he feel panic or calm? How long before the black bliss of oblivion closed over him? Should he exhale and dive down into the depths, filling his lungs with water as he descended? Would he be sucked through the churning propellers? Would someone notice him and try to save him? Would death truly bring an end to his misery? Would anyone find a body? Would finding the body make things easier for his wife? Would there be life insurance? Would there be a tangible end to an intangible life? Would his untimely death ultimately make her life better?

His wife; there was no greater reason to hang on and endure this incredible misery than his love for her. Of course there was his daughter, and his dog, his few friends, some relatives, even the crew on the tug, whose lives would all be affected and altered by the selfish urge that swelled within him almost uncontrollably. 'A fucking manic depressive on a tugboat,' he thought as he rose, looking into the tiny mirror over the sink in his closet-sized cabin. 'Look at yourself. You don't look crazy. How could anyone know by looking into those eyes that you're wrestling with the urge to off yourself, you crazy fuck. What the hell are you doing out here? Why don't you work up some tears, go to the skipper and tell him that you're sorry but you want to kill yourself, could he please let you off somewhere?' The thought of that almost amused him. He knew that out here he had to force himself to maintain control until he broke. He felt very close to that point. 'Get a grip man,' he told himself, 'Just hang on another hour. Get some fresh air, it'll get better. You've been here before and you know it'll pass. Goddamn it, why does it always come back, though? I can talk myself in and out of anything but I can't stop this shit. Is this how the rest of my life is going to go? Fuck! I can't stand the thought of looking forward to much more of this.'

There were tangible symptoms of his affliction. The soaking sweats every time he managed to fall asleep. Waking up feeling more exhausted than when he had gone to bed. Those few minutes of sweet oblivion of sleep wiped out by the inexplicable feelings of terror and utter exhaustion. Then there was the sense of carrying an enormous weight, of trying to swim in molasses, and the choking pressure on his chest that made the act of breathing a misery and a conscious effort. His throat seemed swollen and his whole body felt as if it would begin to vibrate of its own accord. Strange noises seemed to emanate from thin air, and he felt he had little control over his reaction to them or the myriad of disjointed thoughts that raced in and out of his psyche. Even his vision seemed to blur occasionally. He would suddenly become aware of strange smells, both pleasant and awful, and he could not be certain if they were imaginary. He was gripped with waves of nausea and sudden attacks of diarrhoea. He did not feel at ease in any regard. All he wanted was a few precious moments of peace. The only thing that seemed to ease the torture was intense physical activity and he looked forward to getting off the boat to do anything that would allow him to focus outside of the bubble within which he felt trapped. Sweat, pain, and the dynamics of heavy labour were a strange solace at times like this. They kept him distracted, and detached from the secret nightmare reality that only he knew. At home, there were times when he worked maniacally, accomplishing more in a day than others could in a week. He was brilliant and at times could design and create things prolifically. Everyone thought he was gifted; he knew he was driven. At times he would work to the point of near-exhaustive collapse in the hope that he would be able to sleep. It did not work that way, however.

He felt terribly frustrated. There were no visible symptoms that someone else could immediately recognize and it left him feeling utterly alone. Probably only his wife could tell when an attack was upon him. Anyone else with whom he needed to discuss it with had to be told, even his doctor. He always felt like a fool and a sham, although they said nothing to make him feel that way and he was grateful to them for their indulgence and concern on his behalf.

A psychiatrist had once told him that part of the problem with manic depression was that it was trendy to claim to have it, even though most did not. Being unhappy and being a manic depressive were two entirely different things. Although he felt terribly lonely, he actually wanted to isolate himself when he was having an attack, even if it went on for several weeks or months. It was real enough to him, someone whom others regarded as a husky tough-guy with a strong masculine self-esteem, someone with no patience for those would not try to endure. He felt tainted, outcast, dirty and unworthy of even enjoying the comfort of being with his wife. How could he openly tell someone that he was in fact manic depressive and was having an attack?

'What the hell brought it on this time?' he wondered. There never seemed to be any pattern to things. Life had seemed good, smooth, mellow, under control. He felt so good that he had stopped taking the little green and white capsules that the doctor prescribed for him and everything went on beautifully. Then - wham! With no notice, no warning, he was frying in his own juices again, choking, struggling to surface for one more breath, fighting not to dive for the bottom and end everything, everything, everything.

He was thankful that he at least understood the nature of his problem, that it had been identified. He held out hope that the attacks would end eventually. He knew now they were survivable, but there were times when he would get massively depressed and strung out to the point of total irrationality. He had destroyed several relationships, careers and in fact, a good part of his adolescent and adult life, until finally one day his doctor had frankly asked him how often he thought of killing himself. That was the beginning of the acknowledgement of the problem. Things had improved considerably since then, but now here he was back in the same old pattern, feeling lower and more desperate and trapped than ever. If it was going to keep coming back like this, what was the point of going on, dragging himself and others through it all again and again?

Maybe suicide was a logical consideration. The psychiatrist had described suicide as: 'A permanent solution to a temporary problem'. He clung to that witticism and the love and compassion he had been blessed to find in his marriage. It had taken him years to fully accept his wife's love, her unconditional acceptance of him and his fluctuations. The fact that someone he so highly revered held him in this regard helped sustain him through the dark times. He just wished that he did not feel so dependent on her and felt guilty for his weakness. This urge to kill himself had been with him since childhood. He had lived with it all his life and for a long time he assumed that everyone had the same occasional urge. His life had been an emotional roller coaster of highs and lows, a constant of poor self-esteem, a fear of failing and a terror of succeeding. As he grew older, the random patterns of his trauma clung to him like a vivid birthmark. He could not leave the force of his weakness behind him. Now once again he was cursed with a deep depression.

'What *did* bring it on this time?' he wondered. He was not sure that anything caused it, or that it just happened beyond the realm of control or recognition. Recently he had slammed figuratively into a wall in regard to his finances. He was suddenly forced to realize that he was in debt over his head and that the obvious way out was to sell his beloved sailboat. The realization shattered him. If there was something he valued as much as his marriage, it was the sanctuary of his boat, that tangible evidence of his dreams (which helped distract him from the dreariness of his everyday life), and the simple delight of being out on the water, either under sail or anchored peacefully. Sailing was an activity where he felt in control, in harmony with the world around him no matter what happened. Unfortunately, he had managed to turn sailing and his boat into a virtual debtor's prison.

The sailboat had been an ongoing project. He had borrowed money, refinanced and consolidated debts over and over again, but he was always too compulsive and impatient to clear up his finances before forging ahead. While he could not be accused of spending for the sake of it, or of being an addict to buying things, he did achieve a sense of well being from acquiring things that he convinced himself were necessary for the boat or some project at home. He never considered the consequences of buying on credit until he fell into remorse over his thoughtlessness. Then he would be buying something else, and now it was catching up with him once again. It was a weary circle, an endless game of Snakes and Ladders.

He often pondered whether his disorder was learned behaviour or a genetic malfunction that he had inherited. Both his mother and father had suffered severe mood swings, becoming often violent and abusive, compulsive and obsessive, and always going backward with their lives despite a tremendous capacity for hard work. His father had died alone and deeply in debt. His mother, (who had left his father when he was still young) lived alone, and was very lonely, frustrated and bitter, but too anti-social to interact positively even with her own children.

As middle age approached, his physical health was starting to betray him. He was beginning to lose time from work because he kept re-damaging old wounds that had probably been incurred in the first place because of his compulsive, workaholic methods. He was becoming burned out and working at a job that was for men half his age. He was losing more and more income because of that. His working future looked bleak.

Tug boating had seemed a logical thing for him to do. It was a field where he could apply all his other experience and he loved being on the water. He could avoid the eternal stress he had known in the world of business and industry, although he had difficulty accepting that, as a deckhand, he was not able to participate in the decision making of the ship's affairs. However, he reasoned that even though it was a fourth career for him, he could still work his way into becoming a captain with plenty of time to develop a reasonable pension. Unfortunately, the industry was now in a down-sizing transition and there was clearly little hope for him to rise above the present level. It appeared that he may even lose the job that he had. He considered that perhaps a manic depressive would not be suited to being a captain anyway. If you could not control your own emotions, how could you assume the responsibility of a ship and crew? He knew that was an oblique perspective, but in his present state he was unable to consider much in a positive light.

Part of the problem with working on the tugs was the environment that he must assimilate. Once aboard, he never knew how long a trip would last. Only when he arrived at the dock would he learn who his shipmates would be, often people who were not interested in working at being compatible, and who had their own personality disorders of varying degree. It was the type of work which attracted aberrant characters, people who did not fit into the regular routines of society, and it ultimately shaped unconventional behaviour because of the nature of the life style. While at home, he could enjoy two or three weeks of free time, albeit tempered with the wait for the next call to work which you could never anticipate. Tugboats are noisy, hot, smelly, dirty, and often claustrophobic in design. There is nowhere to go and be on one's own. The most valuable aspects of life aboard are sleep and privacy. Often enough, there is precious little of either. It is not an environment for someone subject to severe mood disorders.

Now he lay in his bunk, a narrow coffin-sized box designed to keep a man in place. Sleeping in comfort was irrelevant. He gripped the sides of the bunk partly in an effort to rise and go outside and also to hold himself in place, afraid that he really was about to lose control of his mind and actions. Fighting with himself, castigating himself, he tried not to weep from behind tired, dry eyes that ached from his ordeal of sleeplessness and angst.

He tried to focus on a single thought to displace the madness racing through his brain, and began again to piece together a recognizable scenario that preceded his attacks. He recalled that he had been working fiercely hard and continuously without any leisure time. He had increasing difficulty sleeping, waking with a start and finding the bedding drenched with sweat. The strange dreams had reoccurred, usually forgotten as soon as he awakened, but this time he had one that he could not forget.

He found himself on top of a mountain in a place vaguely familiar, but also surreal and mysterious. However, he could not name the mountain or the town that lay below it across a wide belt of farmland. It strangely resembled an area where he had lived as a child but it was entirely foreign to him. He was working under the guy-wires of a massive radio tower, digging in rocks with a square-nosed spade when he was suddenly overcome with an urge to fly. He flung himself from the edge of a precipice, sitting on the blade of the shovel, astride the handle shaft like a witch on a broom, steering by twisting the grip at the end of the shovel. Suddenly his dog was with him, sitting on the back of the shovel behind him and together they soared and swooped joyously through clouds above the fields so far below. There was a sense of euphoria, of ecstasy and triumph. He could fly simply with the force of his own will power, dependent on no-one or nothing to be free. He reasoned that it was their tremendous forward airspeed that kept them aloft. He had no fear of falling and, bemused by the knowledge that as they glided closer to the ground their speed may well kill them, he flew happily and serenely on. He brought the shovel in low and fast across the leafy, green-treed streets of the town, and then suddenly found himself standing on one of the streets that he had seen from the sky. He was looking up at a sign, Tribute Street, and he felt a deep peace.

It was a scene from the past, sometime in the early 1950's, and he was a time traveler from the future. Immaculate cars and beautifully dressed people flowed serenely past, oblivious to his presence. Suddenly his daughter was by his side and shared his awe as they slowly walked the street lined with massive gleaming cathedrals built of polished black marble and ornately decorated with rare wood and precious metals. His daughter walked away, crossing the street to sit behind the wheel of a huge, gleaming black and chrome Buick convertible. She did not look back as she drove away. He began to tingle and feel very hot, and realized that he was melting like a blob of butter, soaking into the white concrete of the sidewalk where he had stood. Suddenly his dog was beside him again, just as he melted to chin-depth. She whined desperately licked at the spreading stain on the sidewalk. He knew that at least the dog truly had loved him, as his last remaining eye began to dissolve and the world faded into a swirl of blurred colours. Then he awoke drenched in sweat, his wife asleep beside him, breathing softly. He rose from the bed in tears, horrified by the dream and its perversity. Later he returned to bed but was terrified of falling asleep again and returning to the nightmare.

At the time he did not care what the dream might mean, but was concerned that he had experienced it and could remember it so vividly. Now, as he lay in his bunk it replayed clearly through his mind again. He realized that previously he had experienced similar descents into abysmal depression. He hoped now perhaps to discern a recognizable pattern. He would have to pay closer attention in the future and try to recognize the signs: repetitive behaviour, feelings, perceptions that preceded his descent into this one-man hell where he now writhed.

Unable to stay in his bunk a moment more, he rose, grappling with himself for control, putting on a mask that would, he hoped, appear normal to the rest of the crew. There were still three hours until he went back on watch. Desperate to find a way of passing the time, he decided that while all the feelings were fresh and the experience was in progress he would try and record it. Perhaps there would be some value in that, a therapeutic process. He sat at the galley table and began to write. 'He knew he should not be there, it was the worst place in the world for him to be, but he felt he had no choice in the matter.'

Manic Depressive's Prayer

In my late fifties, I still have not beaten it. 'Illegitimi non carborundum.' Don't let the bastards grind you down. But they have. I know what is happening and there is nothing I can do about it. I am just too worn down. The bad luck goes on and on. Every time I get back on my knees, every time I manage to get my leg swung over the wall, with real hope and good possibility nearly within my grasp, something happens to slam me back face-down in the mud.

It took me until I was forty to understand what the problem was. The doctors and psychiatrists have counselled and prescribed. I have lived on their pills for years. I realized the pills were helping me to put on weight. Obesity is often yet another symptom of the disorder and yet another reason it becomes exacerbated. The more depressed you are, the more you are inclined to eat and so the spiral deepens. Compulsive behaviour is a symptom of depression. As long as I feel in control and when things are going the least bit well, I am fine.

Then the skid begins again. This time, it is another goddamned financial crisis. I cannot go ahead, and I cannot stop the imminent crisis that looms a few days ahead. I need a miracle but I know there won't be one. I don't have the strength to hang on until a little light might begin to shine.

I sense that I create my own bad luck. Those who know me swear that I do not and that, in fact, despite the odds, I manage to soldier on, positive every time to the bitter end. Even writing these few words is a positive, tangible effort to redeem the situation and plot a way out. But I see nothing. That is where I am again today, at the bitter fucking end. The weariness, the weight and darkness are back and no one, or nothing, can put the old cracked egg back together. I don't even want to try any more; I am fed up with failure.

People who know me describe me as jovial, possessing a 'wicked sense of humour', a person who can find the bright side in any situation. What a clever, pathetic fraud I am. There are so many times when, despite the mirth, in the middle of the laughter, I really do want to die. The doctor says that if I have made it this far in my life without suicide, then the odds are that I shall manage to survive whatever lies ahead. I am a tough nut.

Fuck him. I really want to put a gun in my mouth and end this. I know what that would do to the ones I love and who love me. That awareness prevents me from being so selfish. However, I just want to go to sleep and never wake up. After all the pain, I crave an exit. I have nothing to contribute. There is no reason for my existence if it is only to endure more of the same. I would even be content to die while saving someone else who could enjoy life. I don't care. Please God, just make it stop.

In a moment of clarity I realize that the urge for suicide is as much about self-determination, and for once being absolutely in control, as it is about the ending of pain. Perhaps the reason I don't actually swallow the pills or French-kiss the twelve-gauge is my fear of somehow messing it up. Life is bad enough now. I am not nearly as afraid of dying as I am of not living. Insecurity rules my life. The existence continues.

Manic Best

People always attempt to do what is apparently, at the time, and to their perception, the very best thing. 'Best' has an infinite number of definitions divided by what is best for oneself and what is best for others. However, even the concept of best for others is ultimately always about what is best for self. Best, in any regard, should not be misinterpreted as 'easiest'. To love, no matter how sacrificially, is a selfish act.

Selfish or unselfish, what is best? When a human being is severely depressed, the perception of best becomes further confused.

There are varying degrees of depression, from a fleeting regret to an overwhelming cerebral dysfunction beyond any possibility of intervention or inspiration. You cannot be 'cheered up' by anyone or anything. Suffering from severe, clinical depression is a force so inexorably beyond the sufferer's control, that no amount of positive reinforcement can alter its course and the only clue the victim has that they have not descended into madness is that they continue to question their sanity.

Others might consider a sufferer to simply be weak-willed, or a dramatic 'Prima Donna'. Motivation always comes from within, but without a sufficient life force it cannot happen.

Imagine riding on the front of a runaway train inside a long, abysmally dark, winding tunnel. Envision clinging to front of the locomotive. Every fibre of your being is aware of the dire peril. The dark suffocating wind rushes past you. You can see nothing. The train roars and clatters. The tiny platform, on which you are clinging, lurches and shudders. There is nothing you can do, although you would do *anything* to end the ride. You believe the only person who can affect change is yourself. With trial and error, a correct medication may shed enough light to allow the victim to clamber back to the engine's controls and, with luck, find and apply the brake. Then, perhaps, the correct lever may be found to back the train all the long way out of the tunnel. There is never a guarantee that the wild ride will not begin again.

Suicide occurs as an act to end the pain and terror and may possibly be a final attempt at being in control. It is what seems best, both selfishly and unselfishly.
It may truly be an effort to rid those you love and who love you of the burden that you see yourself as being. What probably keeps a severely depressed person from suicide is the fear of failure and the lucidity that there are many fates worse than death. What has kept me from suicide is that consideration, as well as knowing what the tragic act would do to those who love me, especially if I botched the attempt.

On this dark day, I try to analyse what the hell is going on in my head and soul. The cold and dark and fog outside are no match for the horror that lives within me. I am fifty-six years old and have lived with this ordeal since childhood. I have written an entire book analyzing my history and still cannot affect a meaningful change. At this point in my life, seeming to be out of control yet again, writing this is my effort of the moment to survive through to the next minute. Logic is attempted as a solution to an emotional problem. I know what my other catharsis is: water - being in it, on it and around it in every way possible. Even having a shower helps. Swimming often gets me through the day. Being on my boat is ultimate bliss, but I have no money to go the pool, let alone go sailing. The frustration and sense of hopelessness tightens the spiral. This latest episode is the worst yet. I tell myself, just as others tell me, that I am not ill. I only suffer from massive self-pity. If everything does not go 'my way' I deliberately hide in my melancholy. But is it an excuse for my failure to find and keep gainful work? No. In fact, to survive one day of this ordeal requires a special strength most do not possess. There are other things I'd rather be doing.

Aware of my life of relative privilege, I have an incredible, wonderful wife, a lovely home, a fine yacht, a beautiful daughter, and a happy little dog. Even with a brilliant, supportive doctor, I cannot get rid of this constricting state I am in. I feel like the proverbial waste of air, useless and hopeless. Yes I am aware of, and cannot imagine, the desperate existence that millions of other people on this planet endure without incessant depressive melodrama. Logic does not work. Yet somehow a faint hope flickers that this can be turned into a useful experience that will qualify me to be a productive, useful citizen. Perhaps I can yet be the loving, supportive, contributing husband I so much want to be. Perhaps there can be a life. Perhaps I can make a positive contribution.

Enough

I have done my best. I have tried to describe to those blessed to live without a permanent depression disorder what it is like inside my dark world. For those who share this curse, I hope I have provided affirmation that you are not alone in your suffering. I realise there is little comfort in that, and admit that my clumsy attempts are a selfish effort to find some degree of peace through self-analysis. It has not worked.

Aware as I am of my condition, its ebbs and floods and swirling currents, I can offer no one any assurances. How I would love to live to the end of my life as a happy, or at least content, man. That seems impossible.

How wonderful it would be to travel through life without fear of being once again possessed by the demon monkeys who so often crowd together on my shoulders and jabber their dark poems and evil denigrations. I know I can never exorcise them permanently, but I would love to be able to recognise their onslaughts well enough in advance to turn and face them, to denounce and repel their horrible influence. Or perhaps they are always there, and at times I am able to acquire the strength to function despite their burden. It seems I am losing that power.

It does not matter. Whatever is left of my life seems bleak. I have not realised one dream. At this point I have almost given up that unique human capacity to visualize what I might achieve and enjoy and share. To dream is the greatest of human attributes. To achieve a dream must be heaven. All I can hope for is peace and the last place I can now hope to find that is within oblivion.

There must be a heaven somewhere because there certainly is a hell.

"Our deepest fear is not that we are inadequate.
Our deepest fear is that we are powerful, beyond measure.
It is our light, not our darkness that frightens us.
We ask ourselves, "Who am I to be brilliant, gorgeous, talented, fabulous?"
Actually, who are you not to be?
You are a child of God.
Your playing small does not serve the world.
There is nothing enlightened about shrinking so that
other people won't feel insecure around you.
We were born to make manifest the glory of God that is within us.
It is in everyone, and, as we let our light shine,
We unconsciously give other people permission to do the same.
As we are liberated from our own fear,
Our presence automatically liberates others."

…..Marianne Williamson (As used within Nelson Mandela's inaugural speech.)

www.ingramcontent.com/pod-product-compliance
Lightning Source LLC
Chambersburg PA
CBHW022354280326
41935CB00007B/181